DAVID
JEREMIAH

WHY *the* NATIVITY?

25 compelling reasons
we celebrate the birth of Jesus

Tyndale House Publishers, Inc., Carol Stream, Illinois

Visit Tyndale's exciting Web site at www.tyndale.com.

Visit David Jeremiah's Web site at www.davidjeremiah.org.

TYNDALE and Tyndale's quill logo are registered trademarks of Tyndale House Publishers, Inc.

Why the Nativity?

Designed by Julie Chen

Edited by Kathryn S. Olson

Published in association with Yates & Yates, LLP, Attorneys and Counselors, Orange, California.

ISBN 978-1-4143-3381-6

Printed in the United States of America

15   14   13   12   11   10   09
7   6   5   4   3   2   1

Though he was very rich, yet for your sakes he became poor, so that by his poverty he could make you rich.

2 CORINTHIANS 8:9

CHRIST CHOSE A STABLE SO THAT HE COULD IDENTIFY WITH THE LEAST OF US, WITH THE POOR AND THE VULNERABLE. HE DEMANDED NONE OF THE WORLD'S COMFORTS NOR PROTECTIONS. JESUS CAME EXPOSED, FROM THE FIRST MOMENT, TO ALL THE DANGERS THE WORLD COULD OFFER, AND SO HE REMAINED UNTIL THEY LED HIM TO THE CROSS. HE CHOSE THE LEAST SO THAT YOU MIGHT HAVE THE MOST. HE ENTERED BY THE STABLE THAT YOU MIGHT DWELL FOREVER IN THE PALACE.

_____

Presented to

_____

By

_____

On the Occasion of

_____

Date

Dedication

To my ten grandchildren—David Todd, Grace Anne, Bradley, Alexandra, Lauren, Ryland, Makenna, Noelle, Hayden, and Luke. May this true story of Christmas remain with you all of your days.

Contents

Acknowledgments

Even after having preached about the miracle of the Incarnation for nearly forty years, I am awestruck anew at the wonderful gift God gave to us in eternal life—and the terrible price that was paid for it. The only real response we can have in view of such love is *why?* The concept for this book, based on that simple one-word question, came from our friends at Tyndale House. Thanks to Ron Beers, Mark Taylor, Ken Petersen, Karen Watson, Carol Traver, and the rest of the editorial staff at Tyndale for their vision and oversight of this book project.

Thanks, too, to my research team of Robert Morgan and William Kruidenier for their insights and observations.

Thanks to gifted editor, writer, and friend Rob Suggs for making himself available in a particularly challenging period in his life and career.

Thanks to my son, David Michael; Paul Joiner; Mary Cayot; and Cathy Lord who also served on the team.

Thanks to my personal assistant at Turning Point, Diane Sutherland, who made my office work around my writing schedule and helped keep me on track for deadlines.

My staff at Shadow Mountain Community Church deserves special thanks for giving me both time and support in the many challenges of such a multifaceted ministry. A special thanks to

Barbara Boucher, who faithfully administrates my office at Shadow Mountain.

Another thank-you goes to my friend and agent, Sealy Yates.

A very special thanks goes to my wife, Donna, without whom I could do none of the things I am called to do in this ministry. Her consistent support and encouragement enable me to be faithful to God's call on my life.

INTRODUCTION

$\mathcal{I}$t's early December, and we're driving home after a tiring day. Stopping at a traffic light at the intersection of Main Street, we have to smile. The town has placed its decorative lights along the parkway, and they shine red and green. The pharmacy window offers a soapy *Season's Greetings* written in red and white candy-cane letters. Several finely manicured trees bear wired lights, and they seem to complete the cheerful scene.

Christmas. As hectic as it has become, we enjoy the inevitability of the season that punctuates each passing year. It brings back those old favorite songs for another encore. We visit extended families and enjoy parties with our friends. As our world keeps roaring into an uncertain future, Christmas is a kind of security blanket that connects us to the past.

The traffic light is green, and we turn onto Main Street. There's the courthouse, dark and empty after another day of civic business. Yet the front lawn offers illumination. As we pass the old World War I statue, we see what is lit: a colorful tableau with the facsimile of a stable, just a bit smaller than life, and the sculpture of a young woman dressed in the ancient garb of the Middle East, who is leaning over to see her baby.

The child sleeps in a little trough, and there are several plaster animals nearby: a donkey, a sheep or two, a cow. The father is there, too, along with a few characters who appear to be shepherds and wealthy Arabian dignitaries, bearing gifts. And above all these things we see the figures of several angels, lit by spotlight and apparently singing.

We drive more slowly as we approach, wanting to take in the spectacle. It's a manger scene, of course. Who wouldn't recognize the familiar characters from the Christmas story? Many of us dressed up as shepherds and wise men once ourselves, gracing the holiday pageants of our schools and churches.

But some other stray thought is causing us to take a second look at the courthouse display. Wasn't there something in the newspaper about this Nativity scene? Yes—we remember now. Some local citizens are protesting the use of the decoration. They say religious imagery should not be displayed on government property. In opposition, of course, are a few pastors and businesspeople who claim that this is a town tradition and that this quiet scene has never offended anyone before.

There's also some kind of hullabaloo over whether stores can have Christmas trees or whether they should be called "holiday trees." Now that we come to think of it, there seem to be strong emotions on every side of this issue of Christmas and the Nativity story. What could possibly be so controversial about Mary and Joseph and their baby? They are simply icons to many people—part of a religious education recalled from childhood, figures on a Christmas card from an old friend. Why the Nativity?

On some impulse, we pull the car over to a parking meter and step into the chilly air. We walk over to the Nativity scene on the courthouse lawn and reflect carefully on what lies before us. For the first time, certain questions suggest themselves. Why was this child born in a stable? Why the shepherds, the angels, the wise men? Why was this woman, Mary, chosen to become one of history's most famous and beloved figures? And what about Joseph?

Most of all, there are questions about the little Child at the very center of the tableau. His birth was, what, two thousand years ago? Jesus was his name, and he was a poor man. From sometime in the past you

AS OUR WORLD KEEPS ROARING INTO AN UNCERTAIN FUTURE, CHRISTMAS IS A KIND OF SECURITY BLANKET THAT CONNECTS US TO THE PAST.

can remember a short essay about him that said this man never traveled outside his own country, never held an office or had a family, and never wrote a single book. Yet it went on to say that all the armies, navies, and kings in history never affected the world as much as this "one solitary life."

Is that true? And if so—*why?*

In this little book, we'll set forth on a quest for answers to that question. It will require doing just what the shepherds did, just what the wise men did, and even what Joseph and Mary did. We need to travel to Bethlehem. Though many years have gone by, and that stable is long gone, we need to concentrate our gaze through the mist of time and look upon that Child whom the shepherds adored. We need to answer all the questions that come to mind about this historic event, which is so dear to the hearts of so many people.

Then, having considered questions about the event itself, we will be left with a final one: *Why should we care?* What does Jesus mean to us? Does the beauty and truth of the Nativity need to be displayed in our own lives, as it is displayed on that courthouse lawn? Or is it just another historic event, just another ancient superstition, a leftover fairy tale from childhood? Let's be prepared to ask the questions, and to find honest and satisfying answers.

This journey will take us to a faraway place and to a time that might otherwise be forgotten. We will need to know a little about the nation Jesus came from, about the Romans who occupied Israel. We'll learn a little more about shepherds and those intriguing wise men.

Let's set our course, then, for two millennia ago—the dividing point of history. The scene is a little town on the quiet landscape of Judea. There are rumors of a miracle happening in the night. Are you ready to investigate?

The shepherds said, "Let's go to Bethlehem! Let's see this thing that has happened, which the Lord has told us about" (Luke 2:15). Consider this your invitation to a remarkable journey to a moment of wonder, deep in the bygone days of the Roman Empire. Are you ready to travel?

WHY THE PROPHECIES?

$\mathcal{T}$ime is a mystery. We live each day immersed in it, so we cannot imagine a life outside of it, looking in. Time marches by us, moment by moment and year by year. It leaves its mark upon us more than we leave our mark upon it.

Imagine standing several miles from a great mountain range. You admire the majestic chain from its foothills in the west to the last outcroppings in the east. But if you didn't have that separation—if you were standing on one of the mountains—you would see only the scenery that was right around you.

God watches over us from outside the straight mountain range that is time. He sees past, present, and future in one unbroken line. And as long as we are travelers through this life, climbing from one slope to the next, we lack his perspective—with one exception, that is: the men and women known as the prophets.

God gives many amazing gifts. To some he gives a surplus of wisdom, to others a specially loving heart. And some have received from him the sight to perceive certain shapes in the mist of the future. Those with this gift have always been people obedient to God and to his purposes. Why would he let them see what was to come? Because he loves us, and he wants us to know what lies ahead, whether for our encouragement or as a sober warning. A prophet's central mission, as a matter of fact, is not to predict but to preach. He speaks more of the present than the future.

Even so, the Old Testament prophets spoke frequently about a coming champion. Every page, from Genesis to Malachi, seems to tremble with the wondrous anticipation of his coming. The books were written by many different writers, at various times over many centuries. What bound the readers and writers together was their identity as a special people that God truly cherished. Through that particular nation, a small one called Israel, God's plan was to let the whole world know of his love.

But that nation encountered times of grief and despair. Because the Israelites occupied one of the most contested areas in all the world, they were frequently under attack by tribes and empires—by the Philistines, then the Babylonians, and finally the Romans. Their walls and homes and Temple were built, destroyed by enemies, and rebuilt.

Finally, Israel became a dying nation, filled with confusion and doubt. It was against that scene that the great age of the prophets came. Many of the Jewish people had been carried away into slavery. Some had lost their sense of national identity in exile. Many were cynical, faithless, embittered. Everyone yearned for the great days of the kings—David and Solomon and all their glory. And it was here that the prophets—men such as Isaiah, Jeremiah, and Micah—urged the people to keep the faith. Their message was, *Wait for one more king. This one will be the greatest of all, and he will end our struggle forever.*

Just when people most needed hope, God sent spokesmen to offer a foretaste of a better future. Throughout the words and work of the prophets, there were glimmers of a savior—a king who would rescue his people and restore them to God. In fact, there were more than three hundred specific prophecies in the Hebrew scriptures about the promised "Messiah," as they called him.

The hints were tantalizing. Isaiah said that this special deliverer would be born of a virgin (see Isaiah 7:14). What kind of man could he be?

JUST WHEN PEOPLE MOST NEEDED HOPE, GOD SENT SPOKESMEN TO OFFER A FORETASTE OF A BETTER FUTURE.

Micah, too, offered a prediction that was specific and startling. He said that the king would be born in the town of Bethlehem. That prophecy reads, "You, O Bethlehem Ephrathah, are only a small village among all the people of Judah. Yet a ruler of Israel will come from you, one whose origins are from the distant past" (Micah 5:2). Again, it was clear that the Messiah would be one who was not confined by the bounds of time. He would come "from the distant past."

There are references to a ministry of teaching, healing, and miracles. This would be a man who would enjoy public favor, then finally be "despised and rejected—a man of sorrows, acquainted with deepest grief" (Isaiah 53:3). There are surprising references to crucifixion by a writer who had never witnessed such a thing (see Psalm 22).

Isaiah would conclude, "He was pierced for our rebellion, crushed for our sins. He was beaten so we could be whole. He was whipped so we could be healed" (Isaiah 53:5). The people of Israel could hope for a better time, including forgiveness by the God they had abandoned. The coming king would prove that God had never abandoned *them*.

Most amazing of all was the coming Messiah's mission. God said, "You will do more than restore the people of Israel to me. I will make you a light to the Gentiles, and you will bring my salvation to the ends of the earth" (Isaiah 49:6).

Can you see the picture that emerges? It was as if many different artists had drawn strange squiggles on paper separately—only to find that when their fragments of art were combined on a single canvas, there was a beautiful portrait of a king we would come to know as Jesus Christ.

Nearly all of the more than three hundred prophecies have already come true (a few remain for our future). Jesus was all that had been foretold, and so much more. One mathematician determined that the odds of one person's fulfilling even sixty specific prophecies are 1 in 1 plus 157 zeros.

Why the prophecies? They show us that even as Jesus was fully a human being like us, he was also "one whose origins are from the distant past." By reading the prophecies we see the entire mountain range in a breathtaking glance;

we behold a magnificent God who works his purposes out through the march of time, patiently but faithfully, down to the smallest detail. We know that this is a God who can be trusted, and this is a Messiah who fulfills every hope in our hearts.

Discussion Questions

◎ Does knowing that Jesus' birth fulfilled prophecies made hundreds of years beforehand affect your life? In what ways?

◎ Which of the six specific prophecies mentioned in this chapter seems the most amazing to you? Why?

For further study: Read the following pairs of Scriptures to discover more prophecies that were fulfilled in Jesus' first advent: Isaiah 9:7 and Luke 1:32-33; Isaiah 53:12 and Matthew 27:38; Zechariah 6:13 and Hebrews 7:24-25.

WHY DID GOD BECOME A MAN?

*I*n the beginning there was God. And, being God, he created.

The creations of God were magnificent. He made a universe of unbounded dimensions, measured out in stars and galaxies. Its size was matched by its vast complexity, in the intricate dance of atom and molecule. The range of his artistry—his color, his sound, his silence—reflected the wealth of his power and love.

But God wanted more than worlds, so he created *life*. He turned to his special world, the earth, and filled it with plants and animals, monstrous and microscopic—a kingdom of moving and breathing and even thinking creatures, all fashioned in wild variety. There were towering, brooding redwood trees that held court for twenty centuries, decorated by mayflies whose life began and ended within a single day.

But God wanted more than life; he wanted *friendship*,

so he created mankind. This would be his crowning work: a manifestation of life that would reflect his own being. Rocks and trees, stars and whales—these were wonderful, but they were not his children. Men and women, as he made them, would be the close-knit family of an infinite God, clothed though they were in flesh and blood. An outrageous idea for communion it was: the perfect, infinite Spirit who is Lord of all, and the tiny, limited creature that calls itself human.

Yet there was love between them until the children of earth stumbled. That's a story for another day, but the truth is that God's children chose disobedience and fled in shame from his presence. Another name for the disobedience was *sin*, and it became an insurmountable barrier between the Creator and his creatures. Men and women knew God as one would regard a distant uncle who was never seen face-to-face.

In certain moments, the children of earth realized how different life could be. One poet looked around him at the beautiful world and reflected:

> *When I look at the night sky and see the work*
> *of your fingers—*
> *the moon and the stars you set in place—*
> *what are people that you should think*
> *about them,*
> *mere mortals that you should care for them?*
> *Yet you made them only a little lower*
> *than God*
> *and crowned them with glory and honor.*
> *Psalm 8:3-5*

The gulf between that eternal Creator and his tiny, incapable children was just too great. As a result, many ignored him completely. The best and most obedient strove gallantly to please him, but the stubborn human strain of disobedience doomed every effort.

The children had no illusions about their weakness. They knew they were lost, and they longed for the Father to whom every instinct drew them. In their wisest moments, they realized that even now, even with all they had done wrong, their distant Father loved them with an everlasting love. It was a hopeless longing all the same, for the separation remained. He was pure and they were stained. How could they ever aspire to the perfection that would make them worthy of him once again? They might as well set to work on a ladder to the moon.

If the children felt their loss so bitterly, how much more severe was the pain in the Father's heart? It was as great as his love was vast. As is true for any parent, his children were his greatest joy. They had failed him time and again, each of them, every

GOD HAD SENT
PROPHETS
MANY TIMES,
BUT NOW HE
WOULD DO
SOMETHING
FAR MORE
SHOCKING.
HE WOULD
LEAVE THE
THRONE
OF HEAVEN—
A KING IN
DISGUISE,
THE LORD OF
THE UNIVERSE
IN HUMAN
SCALE,
THE CREATOR
AMONG HIS
CREATURES.

day—yet his affection for them was undiminished. He loved each child perfectly, boundlessly, as if that little one were his only child.

So the Father yearned through the centuries and the rise and fall of civilizations, never ceasing to reach out to his prodigal family. He did this in every possible way: through the glories of his creation, through the immeasurable gifts he gave them, through the words of prophets and teachers. He dispatched his servants with countless messages that said the same thing in ten thousand ways: "Come home, come home! You are loved now and forever."

The great problem must have a solution. The first order of business was to reintroduce the children to their Father. How could impure flesh know pure Spirit? There must be a way that men and women could know what God is like and, therefore, realize what life can be. The full extent of that, of course, was greater than the capacity of their understanding. For example, they could never comprehend the nature of heaven. To do so, they would need to enter those gates—and in their tainted humanity, they could not do so.

Yet heaven could come to them.

Heaven could not be poured into the stained vessel that was the earth. But there was another way: God himself could make the journey. He could pour his Godhood into flesh and blood and visit the earth as a man himself! He could walk among people as a full-fledged human being in every respect, yet be fully God at the same time. He had sent prophets many times, but now he would do something far more shocking. He would leave the throne of heaven to walk among them—a King in disguise, the Lord of the universe in human scale, the Creator among his creatures.

Then the nature of God would be clear to all. People on earth could see what God was like. They would behold his perfect love and faithfulness, his unbounded devotion even to those who were sick or small or dark hearted. They would know the things that mattered to him. And in that Incarnation, they would see a perfect model of what life could really and truly be.

All of this must happen if God and humanity were ever to be reconciled. So the Lord of the universe invaded this world.

He entered our world through a doorway called Bethlehem, and the world was changed forever.

> *The Word became human and made his home among us. He was full of unfailing love and faithfulness. And we have seen his glory, the glory of the Father's one and only Son.*
>
> *John 1:14*

Discussion Questions

- If you were God, would you have chosen the same method to reach humanity? Why or why not?

- What ways did God use to reveal himself to man before he sent his Son?

For further study: How can people have a relationship with the God of the universe? Read these verses to see God's plan for you: John 3:16; Romans 3:23; Romans 6:23; and Romans 10:9, 13.

WHY
MARY?

*T*he town of Nazareth was remarkably unremarkable. It was much like any number of other villages on the Galilean plain. *Plain?* That was actually a pretty good word for the town.

No one particularly boasted of being a Nazarene. Fewer than two thousand citizens called it home. The Romans kept a regional garrison there, meaning the place was considered more than a little unclean to most Jewish people. And when the town did produce a minor celebrity—a compelling new teacher—the hometown was one strike against him. For example, "'Nazareth!' exclaimed Nathanael. 'Can anything good come from Nazareth?'" (John 1:46). Nathanael, however, was later a follower of the teacher.

Nazareth was Jewish by birthright, Roman by claim, and Greek by influence. It was no more than a quiet town where men attended to their daily work and women their households. If it was excitement you were after, you had to walk four miles up the road to Sepphoris. Now *there* was a city, a *modern* place that kept up to date with the latest in Greek culture.

Did Mary ever walk to Sepphoris? Did she long for a more exciting life? We can't be certain. She seems to have been a typical young lady, in a typical small town in Galilee, just before the first century. That presupposed a quiet life passed in useful service to family and community. How could Mary have known about the life that lay ahead for her? What would she have thought about the divine burden she would carry, the glories she would behold, the loss she would experience?

On that day of days, Mary no doubt turned her efforts to the mundane task of grinding the grain into flour for daily bread. Did she urge a little brother or sister to gather thorns and sticks for the oven? Did she hurry about the rooms of the family home, tidying, dusting, fetching water pots?

These are good guesses, but we can be sure of one subject that held a grip on her imagination. What young girl, from any time or place, wouldn't be preoccupied with her own approaching wedding?

Yes, any girl's most cherished hope was about to be fulfilled in Mary's life. She would be thinking about her young carpenter. She and Joseph may

ON THAT DAY OF DAYS, MARY NO DOUBT TURNED HER EFFORTS TO THE MUNDANE TASK OF GRINDING THE GRAIN INTO FLOUR FOR DAILY BREAD.

have played together in the fields as children. Now they had grown up and were ready to begin adult life. The two sets of parents had arranged a marriage that would unite not just the two young people but the two families. The couple was betrothed, the most binding form of engagement. Legally it meant that Mary was already Joseph's wife, though they could not be together until after the wedding.

What lay ahead for Mary was a whirlwind of happy preparation, perhaps the most enjoyable time of a young lady's entire life. There was the exchanging of gifts by the family; the joy and revelry of the ceremony, with the opportunity to wear jewelry and fine clothes; and finally, of course, she would leave her home—a moment both happy and sad. A Jewish young lady would live with the groom's family, and there the two would begin a life and a family to call their own.

Such hope adds a spring to the step. Mary must have gone about her daily chores with a happy heart. These were her final days as a young maiden.

And then, in the midst of routine and readiness, a single supernatural moment shattered the normality of her life. An angel stood before her, as the first chapter of Luke's Gospel recounts. When did it happen? Perhaps Mary was kneeling beside her bed, attending to prayers, beginning or finishing a day. How frightening the sudden arrival of a heavenly messenger must have been!

"Greetings, favored woman! The Lord is with you," Gabriel said—for it was that particular angel, one of the greatest in God's service (Luke 1:28). Seeing her terror, he assured her there was no reason to fear, for the news he brought was wonderful. God had decided to bless her. She would have a son who should be called Jesus. He would be the Son of the Most High, and he would reign over his people forever.

Such a powerful message is unlikely to take hold quickly. Mary, naturally enough, thought about the practical elements rather than the eternal ones. She wanted to know how it was that a virgin could become pregnant. Gabriel patiently explained that the Holy Spirit would miraculously bring forth a child from her, and this child would be the Son of God.

THE CHILD TODDLED BEHIND HER IN HIS INFANCY. THEN, IN TIME, SHE FOLLOWED BEHIND HIM— ALL THE WAY TO THE CROSS AND THE TOMB.

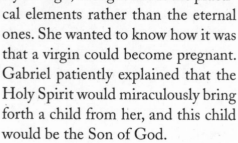

Consider the change that came about in Mary's life. Thoughts of marriage turned to thoughts of motherhood, and thoughts of a quiet, ordinary life turned to the anticipation of being at the center of a spectacular miracle from heaven. No wonder God sent Gabriel himself to help her understand and prepare.

Why Mary? Mary herself must have wondered, *Why am I a "favored woman"? Why me?* Indeed, the reasons she was chosen are known only to God. But it is clear that she was no random selection. Though an ordinary, small-town girl, she must be obedient and courageous, and she was. From her song (see Luke 1:46-55), we know that she was a woman of Scripture, a woman of faith. She must be a virgin, that the glory of God might be miraculously demonstrated. She must be a peasant, in keeping with the humble nature of the Lord's birth.

Mary was all these things. She honored and obeyed the will of her Father, providing his only Son a home from which he would emerge to launch the work that would define all of human history. The Child toddled behind her in his infancy. Then, in time, she followed behind him—all the way to the cross and the tomb.

Mary was favored by God for a task that would finally allow each of us to be favored. Gabriel said, "The Lord is with you," and as a result, the Lord is with us all. In that way, God sent the ultimate Christmas gift not just to Mary but to all of us—and it was Mary who delivered the package.

Discussion Questions

Q Like all Jewish women, Mary surely knew the prophecy of Isaiah 7:14. Why do you think she was still so surprised when Gabriel came to her?

Q When you read the Bible, are you quick to believe and accept its message, like Mary, or do you question and disregard it? Why?

For further study: According to the following Scriptures, what qualifications did Mary have to be the mother of Jesus? Luke 1:27; Luke 1:28, 30; Luke 1:38; and Luke 1:47

WHY THE SONG
OF MARY?

*I*magine for a moment that you have just received the greatest news of your life. Imagine that it came as a personal honor that you would never in your wildest dreams have anticipated.

How would you respond? What would you do? Who would you tell?

Mary, a simple peasant girl, was already looking forward to her greatest day—her own wedding ceremony. Then, without warning, without preparation, she was looking directly into the eyes of an angel. What news did Gabriel bring?

He told her she was in God's favor and that God was with her. This happened to be an era when the children of God felt that their Lord had fallen silent. There seemed to be no more legendary prophets, and the Romans had been allowed to conquer Judea. To hear that God was "present" was remarkable news.

And then Gabriel shared the most amazing information of all: This presence of God would bring about the birth of a child who would be his own Son. This would happen even while Mary remained a virgin. Meanwhile, a "related" miracle occurred: Mary's cousin Elizabeth, elderly and childless, would give birth to a child by her husband. The angel revealed it all.

An immediate surge of self-congratulatory pride would have overcome most of us. We might have reflected on all the superior attributes we possessed and concluded that God had made a good choice! It's human nature. But Mary expressed only her simple obedience: "I am the Lord's servant. May everything you have said about me come true" (Luke 1:38).

Mary must have taken several days to let this life-shaking news sink in, for it was "a few days later" before Luke describes any further action on her part. At that time, Mary did the sensible thing: She hurried to the side of her cousin and fellow expectant mother. Elizabeth lived as much as five days away, probably in the hills surrounding Jerusalem.

When she saw Mary coming, Elizabeth cried out in an expression of joy that demonstrated her understanding of God's actions. Mary, having waited days to share the amazing news that had come into her life, expressed a little joy of her own. And we learn a great deal about Mary from the form that joy took.

Mary lifted her voice in a song of praise to a wonderful God. That song has been cherished through history as the *Magnificat*, which means, "It magnifies." In earlier translations of the Bible, Mary's first words were rendered as,

"My soul doth magnify the Lord." And that's what she proceeded to do. When we magnify, we enlarge or expand upon something. Mary was overjoyed to be in the presence of her cousin, who was obviously like a sister; but she offered that moment of their reunion to the glory of God.

We read these words of Mary's and wonder how an ordinary individual could spontaneously produce such poetry. But here's a secret: Mary was quoting beloved psalms that we can find in the Old Testament. She obviously held them close to her heart. Also, her song of praise is clearly inspired by that of Hannah's, another miraculous mother in Jewish heritage. (See 1 Samuel 2:1-10.) Hannah's child Samuel had become one of Israel's greatest prophets.

WE READ THESE WORDS OF MARY'S AND WONDER HOW AN ORDINARY INDIVIDUAL COULD SPONTANEOUSLY PRODUCE SUCH POETRY.

This song also suggests to us that Mary reflected upon the great characters of biblical history. Hannah may have become her heroine— a woman who dedicated her unborn child to God, then dutifully delivered him to the Temple priest. What a sacrifice! The time would come when Mary would find her own child in the Temple, and she would understand how difficult it can be for a mother to give her child unreservedly to God. Even now, God was strengthening the young woman to whom he would entrust his only Son. Even now, he was preparing her for the tests and trials ahead.

Most of us would like to have known Mary. We'd love

to know more of her inner thoughts. Yet she tells us more about her Lord than about herself. The *Magnificat* offers a wonderful character sketch of our loving Father.

For example, she compares his greatness to her own smallness: "He took notice of his lowly servant girl" (Luke 1:48).

She attends to the greater perspective of God's workings through history: "He shows mercy from generation to generation to all who fear him" (Luke 1:50).

MARY SHOWS EVERY SIGN OF SOMEONE WHO HAS SPENT GENEROUS TIME WITH THE GOD WHO TRANSFORMS ALL THOSE WHO ENCOUNTER HIM.

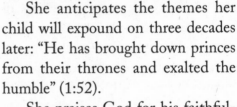

She anticipates the themes her child will expound on three decades later: "He has brought down princes from their thrones and exalted the humble" (1:52).

She praises God for his faithfulness and mercy: "He has helped his servant Israel and remembered to be merciful" (1:54).

Fittingly, her last word is "forever" (1:55). Like so many of the psalms, the Song of Mary soars beyond the limitations of time and space—her heavenly Father is Lord not just of her world, but of all the world; he is Lord not just of her time, but of all human history. She shows every sign of someone who has spent generous time with the God who transforms all those who encounter him.

Why the Song of Mary? It's easy to imagine Mary's journey to be with a good friend who was expecting a miraculous child herself. On the tiring journey, probably in the safety of a caravan, Mary had time to meditate on the goodness of God and the awesome part he had chosen her to play in history. She must have spent a great deal of time in prayer, and she must have searched her memory for every psalm of praise she had planted there. At the beginning of an amazing journey—one no other woman would ever travel—Mary's focus was in the right place. She knew, and expressed through her song, that the resources of God are unlimited. His strength makes all things possible, and his love makes any burden a joy to bear.

Discussion Questions

~ If you were to compose a song of praise to the Lord, what would you tell him?

~ How do you respond when you receive unexpected praise or an opportunity that both excites and frightens you?

For further study: Compare 1 Samuel 2:1-10 with Mary's praise song.

WHY JOSEPH?

*M*ost of our facts about the Nativity came through the skills of two men: Luke and Matthew. These writers wanted to set down the wonderful story of how Jesus first entered our world. Imagine what would have been lost to our understanding and appreciation if someone hadn't preserved the remarkable events of Bethlehem, of the shepherds and wise men, of the inns and the stable.

Without our accounts of the early life of Jesus, we would know almost nothing about Joseph, the quiet adoptive father who protected the infancy of the Savior of the world. Of course, that was a detail our Lord didn't want us to miss. So he sent these two men from different backgrounds and with different goals for their narratives.

Luke, the physician, wanted to write "a careful account" (Luke 1:3) of the life of Jesus and the birth of the church. He wrote his two-volume work, Luke and Acts, for the Greek world. Luke showed a special interest in the women in the life of Jesus. It is clear when we read the Christmas narrative in his Gospel that we are hearing the personal memories of Mary.

Matthew, on the other hand, emphasized the Jewish record, particularly how Jesus fulfilled the ancient prophecies. It was natural that he should seek the testimony of Joseph, the family patriarch, because the Jews were patriarchal people. It was also fortunate that Matthew recorded this precious memory, because Joseph apparently died not too many years later. However long he lived, his life was well spent in invaluable service to God and to human history. He is the "forgotten man" of the greatest story ever told, and it pays us to take a moment to remember him.

Joseph was a carpenter and, as such, most probably a simple and practical man. He would have liked the feel of wood and stone, the satisfaction of building something sound and useful. We can imagine that, like Mary, he envisioned an orderly and ordinary life. He would pursue his craft, maintain a good name in the community, attend the synagogue, and raise a family.

Certainly Joseph's life was proceeding in that direction as he prepared for his wedding. In Jewish culture, unlike our own, the groom was the focus of a wedding. Joseph must have looked forward to the celebration and the simple life that would follow, of taking Mary into his household, of having children. The carpenter was fashioning a well-constructed life.

And then came the dream.

Remarkably, there were to be four supernatural dreams in Joseph's life. The first came at a time of anger and humiliation. In shock and disbelief, Joseph had observed the obvious pregnancy of his fiancée. Mary was expected to be a virgin, and premarital motherhood would be a public scandal. Everyone would wrongly assume that Joseph was the father. Yet Matthew tells us that Joseph's intention was to gently break off the engagement—a reasonable, gracious response in such a crisis. He was practical, but he was sensitive even so.

However, in a dream, an angel instructed him to be faithful to Mary: "'Joseph, son of David,' the angel said, 'do not be afraid to take Mary as your wife. For the child within her was conceived by the Holy Spirit. And she will have a son, and you are to name him Jesus, for he will save his people from their sins'" (Matthew 1:20-21).

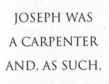

JOSEPH WAS A CARPENTER AND, AS SUCH, MOST PROBABLY A SIMPLE AND PRACTICAL MAN.

Matthew says, in the next verse, that this happened in order "to fulfill the Lord's message through his prophet." But Joseph wasn't accustomed to reckoning upon the old, dusty scrolls. Imagine his difficulty in accepting the brand-new state of affairs that God had laid before him. Not only had he seen an angel—he had seen him in a *dream*. A good carpenter understands what he can touch and feel with his hands. He likes order, predictability, and a product whose craftsmanship can be inspected. Now his world was redefined by something intangible.

Assuming this child was truly the Messiah, how soon

would that be clear to those who laughed and jeered? How was Joseph supposed to parent a future king? And what kind of wife was he marrying, anyway?

There would be more dreams for Joseph in time: to flee to Egypt with his little family; to return again; and finally, to establish a home back in Nazareth, where the child would be safe. The man of wood and stone had to become a man of dream and destiny. The man who had yearned for his own flesh and blood found his calling as an adoptive father.

THE MAN OF WOOD AND STONE HAD TO BECOME A MAN OF DREAM AND DESTINY. THE MAN WHO HAD YEARNED FOR HIS OWN FLESH AND BLOOD FOUND HIS CALLING AS AN ADOPTIVE FATHER.

But these trade-offs were not without benefit. The child who grew toward manhood in Joseph's care, who honored his trade of carpentry, was worth any sacrifice. Today, we know Joseph's name because of his faithfulness and obedience in following every instruction that God gave him. In Joseph and in Mary, God selected the only man and the only woman in this world to whom he would entrust his own precious Son.

Joseph was a quiet man. When the wise men visited, for example, no word is recorded from Joseph. But he was a man of faith, dependability, and practicality who served as a model not only for the beloved Child but for all of us who would stand quietly in that Child's presence.

Why Joseph? To fulfill his plan, God needed a carpenter. He needed a man who was sturdy, stable, and practical, yet sensitive to the voice of God. He needed one who would stand quietly with a young virgin who might have seemed an object of ridicule, yet who carried in her womb the hope of the world. Joseph was strong but compassionate; he was able to lead the tiring expedition to Bethlehem and to the stable, to love and encourage the mother of Christ. Joseph, as the man of the house, was the teacher to give Jesus his first lessons in the law of God. And in Jerusalem, when the boy was twelve and it became evident that his first allegiance must be to another Father, Joseph was the man to humbly and silently step back and let God step forward.

Discussion Questions

⌒ Have you ever been disappointed or hurt by someone you loved and trusted? How did you react?

⌒ Is there someone in your life you have treated as if forgotten? What could you do today to change that situation?

For further study: Read Matthew 1:18–2:23 and list the things Joseph did following each instruction.

WHY DID JESUS COME WHEN HE DID?

*I*magine this scenario: A world leader plans to send a man on a mission of the utmost urgency. The fate of the world rests upon the success of this operation. So the commander thinks carefully, strategically, about his plan. Nothing can be left to chance; every detail must be carefully considered.

The leader will send only the perfect candidate for his mission. He must decide where to deploy his agent, how to get him there, and what goals should be attempted. And timing means everything. If the mission goes into operation too soon or too late, everything will be lost.

The ultimate World Leader—the one at the very top of the chain—planned just such a mission. The world was headed for destruction from the inside out, because humanity was enslaved by the sin in every human being. Men and women were at war with themselves and with one another.

God's response to our hopeless situation is best summarized in these words: "For God loved the world so much that he gave his one and only Son, so that everyone who believes in him will not perish but have eternal life" (John 3:16). Jesus was not only God's Son, but his agent to rescue a lost world. And to succeed, this agent would be required to lay the ultimate sacrifice upon the altar of his world.

Would you agree that God, knowing the cost, would consider every angle in planning such an operation? He sent the right man for the mission, which was accomplished in the only possible way: Jesus' death and resurrection. But what about the timing? Could God have sent his Son earlier or later? Galatians 4:4 phrases the idea beautifully: "When the fullness of the time had come, God sent forth His Son" (NKJV). In other words, conditions were optimal on the battlefield of earth. But why? What was it about the vast Roman Empire that was so ideal for the coming of Christ?

The Romans themselves were part of the answer. For the first time in history, the Mediterranean world—the cradle of civilization—was unified. Alexander the Great, a Greek, had been the first to bridge so many nations, but the Romans had built a foundation that would last longer. They had constructed the famous Roman roads ("All roads lead to Rome") that would allow messengers to travel safely with news and ideas, as Paul and the first missionaries would do. Ships, too, had come of age. Egypt and Italy, Syria and Spain—so many nations shared the "highway" that the Mediterranean Sea had become. Here was yet another means for the message of Christ to spread far and wide.

There was also the *Pax Romana*—the "Roman peace" that endured from 27 BC until AD 180. Jesus was born in the same generation in which it began, and it meant a relatively calm environment for the lower regions of Europe, Asia Minor, the Middle East, Egypt, and northern Africa.

In a city such as Jerusalem, for example, the Jews were allowed to preserve their own faith and customs. The Romans were permissive about religions as long as there wasn't any trouble and the Jews paid a punitive tax—*fiscus Judaicus.*

MANY OTHER IDEAS WERE PRESENT IN THE WORLD OF THE FIRST CENTURY. . . . BUT NO OTHER IDEA WAS CAPABLE OF TOPPLING THE GREATEST EMPIRE IN THE HISTORY OF HUMANITY.

Stability and relative tolerance opened the world to the spread of a new idea; roads and shipping lanes made it happen quickly and efficiently. But there was another key factor: *language.*

The Romans had taken efficient control of much of the known world, but they were still overshadowed by their Greek predecessors in one respect: For many years, people almost everywhere continued to speak Greek. Hellenic Greek happened to be one of the most beautiful and articulate

tongues the world has known. It seemed custom built for the ideas that distinguished Christian life and thought. Would the world have learned Hebrew in order to consider the claims of Christ? It's hard to imagine. But the shared language, Greek, made it possible for Paul and others to travel to many countries and tell people the good news of the gospel without cumbersome translation.

We consider all these factors, and still we are left with an unlikelihood. After all, many other ideas were present in the world of the first century. All of them had Roman roads and peace at their disposal, along with the Greek language. But no other idea was capable of toppling the greatest empire in the history of humanity.

Consider this: An obscure teacher from a small town in a ruined country changed the world—*after his death*. On the Friday of his execution, his followers largely abandoned him. Yet within a generation, he was worshiped in many foreign countries. Within three centuries, his faith was the official doctrine of the empire. And today, 2.1 billion men, women, and children follow that same teacher who was put to death as a criminal.

Jesus indeed came at the perfect time, but he also brought the perfect message. He brought hope and light. In a world ruled by the sword, this teacher spoke of perfect peace. In a world of violence and retribution, he spoke of loving one's enemies. In a world of death, he offered hope of new life—for now and for beyond the grave. The Romans dominated through the power of terror, lifting high a cross that performed its deadly task with unimaginable pain. Jesus accepted that cross, submitted himself to it, and lifted it high as a bridge from the grief of earth to the joy of heaven—and that bridge, he made it clear, was available even to those who persecuted him.

That was a message to capture a world. In the fullness of time, just when his truth and love could spread with greatest impact, Jesus came to bring the most radical, most wonderful message that has ever been presented. What began in a stable in little Bethlehem would redefine history—at the perfect time, and for all time.

Discussion Questions

- Have you ever failed to plan well for an important meeting, assignment, or test? What was the result?

- What new thing did you learn in this chapter about God's careful planning for the Nativity?

For further study: Galatians 4:4 refers to Jesus' incarnation, while Galatians 4:5-7 tells more about God's plan. Read these verses and list other details of God's purpose in sending his Son.

WHY ELIZABETH AND ZECHARIAH'S MIRACLE BABY?

*F*or the people of Israel, the greatest of all legacies was that of having and raising children. In that respect, they were like most of us. In those early days, they found it hard to understand infertility. Many believed that if God was withholding the blessing of children, someone must have done something wrong. And the finger of blame was generally pointed at the woman. She was suspected of some hidden sin, and as long as the childlessness continued, she must still be guilty.

It's hard for us to imagine the lonely spiritual journey of a frustrated, would-be mother during Bible times. *What have I done wrong, Lord? Why won't you reveal my sin so I can atone for it?*

Elizabeth, who lived near Jerusalem, must have prayed those words through her tears on many sleepless nights. Zechariah, her husband, was a priest! It made their problem even more noticeable. There would be whispering about a priest's wife who could find no favor in God's eyes. How Elizabeth must have longed for a daughter to help with the cooking and cleaning, and one day to give away as a bride. Zechariah would have wanted a son, just like any father.

MANY BELIEVED THAT IF GOD WAS WITHHOLDING THE BLESSING OF CHILDREN, SOMEONE MUST HAVE DONE SOMETHING WRONG. AND THE FINGER OF BLAME WAS GENERALLY POINTED AT THE WOMAN.

But the nights were long and God was silent and the crib was empty. Years passed, and the time of gray hair and tired bones crept inexorably nearer. The couple had long since given up hope of children when, unbeknown to them, the time approached for the world's most wonderful event and their amazing part in it.

Luke begins his Gospel with its saga of Christ and Christianity not with Mary and Joseph, not with Herod, but with this very story. Zechariah the priest was in the Temple burning incense before the Lord when suddenly he wondered if he had fallen into a daydream. There, standing to the right of the incense altar, stood an angel! He was terrified, as people always were when an angel came to visit.

The visitor revealed news that was too wonderful to imagine. God would answer years and years of prayers with a child for the couple. Not only that, it would be as if the child himself would reflect the sum total of these years of grief and yearning. He would be a special child, "filled with the Holy Spirit, even before his birth" (Luke 1:15). This was something more than remarkable. For hundreds of years there had been no prophets, and this child would bear the presence of the Lord even in his mother's womb!

The priest may have fallen to his knees, his frame racked by weeping—tears of uncomprehending awe. The angel had gone into considerable detail about the child's future. Neither Mary nor Joseph heard quite so many facts about their coming child.

First of all, said the angel, many people would rejoice with the couple—blessed vindication after so many years of social judgment. The child was to be named John; he would bear the spirit and power of Elijah, that most beloved of prophets; and he would turn scores of Israelites back to the God they had forsaken. He would "turn the hearts of the fathers to their children" (Luke 1:17). Greatest of all, he would prepare the way for the coming of the Lord, just as Isaiah had foretold.

We know him as John the Baptist.

A sudden flash of doubt must have passed through Zechariah's mind. As a priest he knew the prophecies of the coming of one like Moses, one who would announce the Messiah's presence among men. But he lacked the faith to believe. He questioned how this could be true.

The angel then revealed his identity. He was *Gabriel*, who stands at the very throne of God—*Gabriel*, who had visited Daniel and would also visit Mary. And as a mild discipline, he stilled the priest's tongue, so that he could not speak from then until the angel's words were verified. For the first time, he would have something to talk about, and he couldn't utter a word!

Can you imagine his mixture of joy and frustration when he returned to Elizabeth? Indeed Luke tells us that his wife was taken by surprise when the pregnancy came. God "has taken away my disgrace," she said (Luke 1:25).

She was at the beginning of her third trimester when Gabriel made another earthly visit, this time to Mary. Along with the announcement of Jesus, Gabriel let Mary know that her cousin Elizabeth also had some good news: The destinies of their children would be intertwined. Both were miracle births, both fulfillments of ancient words. Unlike Zechariah, Mary had simple faith to believe the angel's amazing news.

GOD IS LISTENING TO OUR PRAYERS, HE IS FAITHFUL TO HIS WORD, AND HE IS PREPARING THE WAY FOR SOMETHING MORE WONDERFUL THAN WE CAN IMAGINE.

When Mary came rushing into the arms of her cousin, the child inside Elizabeth leaped for joy. Mary sang a psalm of praise, quoting Hannah, a famous mother who had also given birth to a prophet after oceans of tears. Mary and Elizabeth, sisters in miraculous grace, held each other close. Mary's news was the greatest; it revealed that the Son of God was to appear. But Elizabeth's news was wonderful, too, for it revealed that the promised herald of God's Son was about to be born—the one God chose to be a shining lamp that would attract people to Jesus, the Light of the world.

When the child came, so did Zechariah's speech. He

offered a song of praise to match those of the women. Another song, of sorts, was later sung about John; this one by Jesus himself. He called this miracle child of Elizabeth and Zechariah the greatest man (see Matthew 11:11) and more than a prophet (see Luke 7:26-28).

The faithless priest and his wife show us that God is listening to our prayers, he is faithful to his Word, and he is preparing the way for something more wonderful than we can imagine. And he rewards even feeble faith.

Discussion Questions

◎ What are you longing for that seems far out of reach? Are you trying to make it happen, at all costs, or are you willing to let it go?

◎ Have you had a season of doubt about God's promises to you? How did you remedy it?

For further study: Read Genesis 18:1-15 for another record of a promised miracle baby. How did the parents in this account react?

WHY BETHLEHEM?

$\mathscr{B}$ethlehem played host to the Nativity, an event that the world hardly noticed, yet that changed the destiny of every human creature. As Ralph W. Sockman once phrased it, "The hinge of history is on the door of a Bethlehem stable."

We imagine a silent night—but remember, the inns were full and celebrants must have roamed the streets. We imagine an obscure town—yet Bethlehem already bore a surprisingly mixed legacy.

The Bible tells us that it was in Bethlehem, for example, that Jacob's beloved wife, Rachel, was buried. Tragically, she died in childbirth as Joseph's beloved brother, Benjamin, came into the world.

Around another bend of history's trail lies Ruth, whose story is short but moving. Two widows—Ruth and Naomi, her mother-in-law—left foreign Moab for the small town where Naomi and her husband had lived, the town of Bethlehem. There they prospered and Ruth remarried. In

Ruth 4, the people offered their blessing on Ruth and her new husband. They compared her to Rachel and expressed their prayers that her descendants would be great.

Those prayers were answered in ways the people could never have dreamed.

Little Bethlehem also provided ancient Israel its most enduring hero. The prophet Samuel had come to town in search of a future king, just as other wise men would do hundreds of years later. The book of 1 Samuel records how the prophet came to the house of Jesse and carefully sized up the young men of the household, one by one. His godly eye finally fell upon David, the shepherd boy, the "least likely to succeed." Here, Samuel announced, was the raw material of a popular king. Here stood one who was destined to be known as the "man after God's own heart." Shepherd to king? The idea was startling.

In darker times, an aging King David would see Israel's mortal enemy, the Philistines, place a garrison in his beloved Bethlehem. When David longed for water from its well, a squad of his courageous soldiers broke through to steal a drink for him—only to see him pour out the water as a sacrifice before God.

The family tree of Jesus Christ shows all three names: Rachel, Ruth, David. Mother, Moabitess, monarch. We cannot help but see the puzzle pieces, the tantalizing clues to the wonderful legacy that would one day belong to Bethlehem.

The greatest clue of all, though, was in plain sight for every Hebrew who searched the Scriptures. In the scrolls of the prophets was written an amazing prediction: "You, O Bethlehem Ephrathah, are only a small village among all the people of Judah. Yet a ruler of Israel will come from you, one whose origins are from the distant past" (Micah 5:2).

Bethlehem Ephrathah—two names, two meanings. *Bethlehem* means "the house of bread." Its Child would later call himself "the Bread of life," and he would say, "I am the living bread that came down from heaven" (John 6:51). What more fitting place than the "house of bread" for such a one to be born?

What about that second name? *Ephrathah*, a much older name for the town, means "fruitfulness." *Ephrath* is a verb meaning "to be fruitful." Once again, the Child of Bethlehem would remind us of his first home when he said, "When you produce much fruit, you are my true disciples" (John 15:8).

THE CLUES WERE ALWAYS THERE—IN THE HISTORY, THE NAMES, AND THE SURPRISING WAYS OF GOD HIMSELF.

For those who read the ancient writings and those who thought about the eternal workings of God, the clues were always there—in the history, the names, and the surprising ways of God himself. That Bethlehem, it bore watching. So as the years went by, the rabbis remembered and the scholars kept an eye on the little town. Everyone else passed it by without much notice, so that upon that amazing night, when a peasant and his betrothed wife stole wearily into town, no one could have anticipated that the world would be changed forever.

Perhaps this is the reason we think of Bethlehem as a timeless town, set on an eternally silent and starry night.

We know that the local inns had room for anyone and everyone but a king; that not so much as a pillow could be offered to one who would one day give all that he had for them. Yet we cannot bear the innkeepers and tax takers much of a grudge—there is too much joy in the occasion.

For in some forgotten corner of a forgotten town in a forgotten country, the most unforgettable news is suddenly abroad. In the "house of bread," the Bread of life has been served for all humanity. In the town of fruitfulness, someone has come to offer the sweet fruit of heaven. And from the place where there was once a well that a thirsty king coveted, there would spring up a fountain of living water for all people. The one who offered it said, "Those who drink the water I give will never be thirsty again. It becomes a fresh, bubbling spring within them, giving them eternal life" (John 4:14).

Why Bethlehem? Why your heart or mine? City and soul, they are equally silent, equally mixed in their histories, equally thirsty. Just as the Child quietly arrived in that town of towns, he longs to be born again in the hearts of every one of us.

Discussion Questions

- Is there a special location associated with your family's history? Have you visited there recently?

- According to this chapter, what other important things happened in Bethlehem?

For further study: Read 1 Samuel 16:1-13. List three interesting things that happened in Bethlehem in this account.

WHY WAS THERE NO ROOM IN THE INN?

$\mathscr{B}$ethlehem was a quiet and uneventful village, little more than a suburb of thriving, cosmopolitan Jerusalem. It wasn't a travel destination as much as a small rest stop on the access road. It was just five miles outside of the big city, where the presence of God dwelt in the Temple. Better lodgings were a matter of merely another hour's walk. Everyone was eager to see Jerusalem—too eager to linger here on the outskirts.

But now the empire was taking names, and all those Israelites who descended from King David were instructed to report to their hometown of Bethlehem. David's time, the glory days of Israel, was now ten centuries in the past, and the late king's extended family constituted a small nation in itself.

Why would the Roman Empire bother about the roll call of a conquered people? As you might guess, it was all about money. Caesar had a healthy interest in keeping the gold flowing Romeward. He wanted a careful and organized count, to make sure every eligible soul paid every due cent.

Therefore, on this wonderful day all roads led to Bethlehem. The little town was overrun with aunts and uncles and cousins many times removed. The scene was a cross between a great family reunion and a business convention. Even with the makeshift inns and hostels that surely sprang up overnight, there was no way Bethlehem could produce the beds it needed. Late-coming travelers were bound to be disappointed.

Envision those jammed avenues! The census was a boom time for innkeepers and food vendors, but also for pickpockets and criminals who could disappear into the crowds. Travelers and raucous music spilled from the doors of taverns, and women of ill repute waited in alleys. The pious and the wicked brushed shoulders. This, then, was the setting for the coming of our Lord.

But consider this: How much thicker would those crowds have been if the world had known what we know? The irony is that thousands of people bustled into town for the world's most wonderful day, all unaware that they were at Ground Zero of a heavenly invasion. They thought they had come for something as bland and uninspiring as tax registration. On the world's first Christmas, they had come to give, not to receive. Hundreds of families must have walked by that stable. They must have passed the mother and her newborn child without a "good morning" or a curious glance. Surely they turned up their noses at the excited but unwashed shepherds who brushed by them on the way to the stable.

God's greatest gift came wrapped in mystery, so that no

one knew what was inside. The Son of God was born into this world; eternity infiltrated time and space. Why, then, was there no room in the inn? If God could mobilize a star from a distant galaxy to invite wise men from the East, couldn't he make one humble room available?

We can't doubt it for a second. This event was no momentary impulse. It was the decisive moment in human history. God had been lovingly planning it since before Creation, and he did not overlook any detail.

The Lord of Creation chose to enter this world quietly amid an unquiet scene. It was by heavenly design that he came into the world not in the relative comfort of the inn but in some farmer's seedy shed. A homeless birth was part and parcel of a homeless life.

His mother, a Nazarene, just happened to be in Bethlehem when her child arrived—as Micah the prophet had foretold. Mary and Joseph took the Child to Egypt for safety, then to Nazareth—after the warning of an angel not to return to the vicinity of Bethlehem. We know that Jesus grew to manhood in Nazareth, but the Scriptures hurry past that period. When we see him at twelve, even then he is on the road to Jerusalem and the Temple. Never do we find him at home.

A HOMELESS BIRTH WAS PART AND PARCEL OF A HOMELESS LIFE.

One day, when Jesus was an adult, a teacher declared that he would follow the Master anywhere. The Lord's reply: "Foxes have dens to live in, and birds have nests, but the Son of Man has no place even to lay his head" (Luke 9:58). His words bear a touch of wistful sadness. The life of Jesus was a long road that began at the stable and led to the cross—and finally, of course, to an empty tomb. The comforts of domestic life weren't possible, for there was work to be done.

Accepting humanity's rejection even in his birth, Jesus sent a message of stubborn, unbreakable love to the world. We would not afford him so much as a cramped closet; we had no room for him, no time to stop and worship, no interest in a peasant child. But that same Child came to find room for *us*. He would, one day, reserve accommodations for each of his own children at the Inn that awaits us on eternal shores.

Before leaving on that final journey, he told his disciples, "There is more than enough room in my Father's home. If this were not so, would I have told you that I am going to prepare a place for you?" (John 14:2). Homeless no more, he would throw open the doors of heaven, so that no one might be left in the cold.

Discussion Questions

◌ When you travel, do you prefer to book reservations in advance or take your chances? Why?

◌ Have you ever been "bumped" from a flight against your will? Have you ever gone to a hotel, having guaranteed your reservation, only to find the hotel overbooked? How did you handle the situation?

For further study: Read John 14:1-3. What does Jesus say he will do after he has prepared a place for us? How can we be certain of our "reservation"?

*W*e cannot be certain whether the birthplace of the Christ child was a wooden shed or an ancient cave. The word *stable* is not found in the Nativity narrative. It's natural to assume such because Luke tells us that the shepherds were to seek the Child "lying in a manger," which was a feeding trough for animals. That trough is actually mentioned twice—once by Luke, and once in the words of the angel who appeared to the shepherds.

First-century Roman reports mention a cave that was believed to be the birthplace of Jesus, and certainly animals were often sheltered in caves. Wouldn't it be wonderful to imagine that in this very shelter David had rested with his sheep many years earlier? He might have composed the Shepherd Psalm on the very spot where the Good Shepherd entered this world. On another occasion, he might have rested here while he received the inspiration to write the Twenty-Second Psalm, which so vividly describes the pain of crucifixion.

All this is simply speculation, of course. What we can be certain about is that Jesus, David's descendant, was born somewhere nearby in an unspecified stable arranged for animals, and that image compels us to worship during the holiday season. It makes a fine picture for our Christmas cards and Nativity sets, with the animals and shepherds and with moonlight reflecting softly on the Child's face.

Many of us haven't visited a barn for a while. The aroma is anything but holy, hay makes us sneeze, and insects abound. Joseph and Mary would have preferred a room in the inn. In a town overstuffed with strangers, a stable offered neither safety nor solitude. The couple needed a restful spot after a weary journey of several days. Joseph worried about his wife, who was obviously due to deliver at any time; he had brought her on such a trip because she was too precious to allow out of his sight. The angel had charged him to care for her, and he was determined to hover over her and fill her every need as the time came for her to deliver.

And so it happened: The Son of God came to this earth in the presence not of world leaders but of animals. He arrived not in a palace or a shrine but in a stable. The Roman emperor Hadrian would later try to send a message of intimidation by covering its holiness with an insulting pagan shrine, but he missed the message that had already been sent. Jesus had forever covered all our anger, all our embattled pride, with love and forgiveness. He came for Hadrian as well as for Mary, for Joseph, for the shepherds and the wise men and those who held the nails that would pierce his hands and feet. The power of his love would melt any paltry insult that tried to cover it.

Ironically, the site traditionally believed to be that of the stable in which Christ was born has become a battlefield of sorts. By AD 135, the Romans were at their wits' end with ongoing riots in the Judean provinces. The emperor Hadrian decided to send a ruthless message by desecrating the local places that Jews and Christians held to be sacred.

The emperor's scouts told him about an interesting cave in Bethlehem, of all places. Local legend insisted that here Jesus, the founder of the Christian movement, had been born in the company of barnyard animals. To make things stranger, this "king" had been executed as a criminal years later. Yet his followers exalted him. Hadrian's men located the cave and erected a temple to Jupiter and Venus over it. *That will show them,* he thought.

Hadrian faded into history, but Christianity proved resilient. Exactly two centuries later, in AD 335, the emperor Constantine visited the site himself. He pulled down the remains of the pagan construction and built a Christian church in its place.

Years later, the Persians knocked down Constantine's church; Christians rebuilt it. Then came the Turks to knock it down again. Then rose the Church of the Nativity, which stands today. Its foundation was laid during the Middle Ages by Crusaders, with their bloody legacy. As recently as 2002, armed Palestinian militants broke into and occupied the church for thirty-nine days. Israeli army snipers killed seven militants and wounded more than forty others, and a destructive fire was set at the place where the holy Child was said to have been born.

What may be the site of the Nativity, then, has become

a center for blood and strife. Even at peace, the great, imposing chapel in Bethlehem is a far cry from the humble stable where the Son of God entered the world. He came in simplicity, not extravagance. He came to bring peace to the world and to reconcile his children in love, not to launch new struggles between us. The very site has become a case in point, demonstrating why we needed Jesus in the first place.

So unassuming was that birthplace that we can't be entirely certain of its exact whereabouts. The site of the present church has been pointed out since the first century, so there's reason to give it credence. Yet do we really need to know where he was born? The true cradle is in our hearts. Whatever men could construct on that site, men could also tear down. But what the Lord brought to us there can never be destroyed.

JESUS CAME EXPOSED, FROM THE FIRST MOMENT, TO ALL THE DANGERS THE WORLD COULD OFFER.

Why the stable? Christ chose a stable in order to identify with the least of us, with the poor and the vulnerable. He demanded none of the world's comforts nor protections. Jesus came exposed, from the first moment, to all the dangers the world could offer, and so he remained until they led him to the cross.

"You know the generous grace of our Lord Jesus Christ," Paul the apostle would write. "Though he was rich, yet for your sakes he became poor, so that by his poverty he could make you rich" (2 Corinthians 8:9).

Jesus chose the least so that you might have the most. He entered by the stable that you might dwell forever in the palace.

Discussion Questions

⊙ Where were you born: in a hospital, a home, or maybe even a car? Why there?

⊙ What are the sights, sounds, and smells of a barn? Can you imagine giving birth to an infant in those conditions? Why or why not?

For further study: Read Luke 2:22-24 and Leviticus 12:2-8. How do we know that Jesus' family was used to a humble lifestyle?

WHY CALL HIM JESUS?

*J*uliet was speaking of Romeo when she asked the famous question, "What's in a name?" Juliet went on to say that a rose by any other name would smell just as sweet. Rename it as you will, a rose will retain its beauty and its fragrance.

She had a point. Isn't a name simply a collection of alphabet letters? If we can't judge a book by its cover, surely we can't judge men or women by their names.

Doesn't this principle apply also to the name of Jesus? It is not what we call him that matters, but who he is. The name provides him with no power, but he certainly empowers the name.

That name is a matter of five little letters in the English language. And yet, as an old gospel song phrased it, there's something about that name. Of all the titles and designations for Jesus that are given by the Scriptures (seven hundred of them according to some counts), *Jesus* is the name we use the most, the one we invoke in prayer, and the one the world recognizes. There is certainly power in the name—power, comfort, and authority.

At the time of his birth, the name of Jesus was in no way unique. In fact, it was a popular name for boys. *Jesus* is just the Greek equivalent of *Joshua*, which means "God saves." It recalled the great leader of Israel who succeeded Moses, leading the Israelites into their Promised Land. For Hebrew families, giving a son that name was paying homage to a national hero, much like George Washington or Abraham Lincoln for Americans. But it also carried the timeless message that "God saves": He holds the answer to every problem.

It's not surprising, then, that the name of Joshua/Jesus was so popular. The Jewish historian Josephus detailed twenty men of distinction known by the name of Jesus, ten of them being contemporaries of the child of Mary.

During the lifetime of Christ, that name continued in popularity until a few years after his death and resurrection. Then, all of a sudden, the name of Jesus disappeared from histories and censuses. Why? Because it had taken on a brand-new and controversial meaning. Christians believed that no child was worthy to bear the name that is above all names. And for nonbelieving Hebrews, the name evoked an influence they didn't embrace.

Whose idea was it to call the Child Jesus? The word came from God himself. Like any father, he wanted to name his own Son. As Joseph slept, an angel came in a dream, giving him assurance, encouragement, and instruction. Remember, Joseph was coping with the shock of finding his fiancée to be expecting a child that he knew wasn't his. He felt the anger and disgrace any young man would have felt. Then the words of God's messenger changed everything. "Do not be afraid to take Mary as your wife. For the child within her was conceived by the Holy Spirit. And she will have a son, and you are to name him Jesus, for he will save his people from their sins" (Matthew 1:21).

Angels, of course, bear dispatches from heaven. This one conveyed the specific desire of God for naming the boy—and *why*. The reason for the name *Jesus* was that "he will save his people from their sins."

The name, then, bore the mission statement: one of salvation for the bearer's people. So many parents bless their children with names for that very reason. My name, David Paul Jeremiah, brings with it an ambitious legacy! It is a constant reminder to me of a king, an evangelist, and a prophet. It didn't take me long to find out that if my name is a mission statement, I can never hope to be fully worthy of it.

But the name of Jesus is different. It says to us, *mission accomplished.* We could never find words to state more simply or more powerfully what Jesus means to us and all that he has done for us. Think of it this way:

IF YOU HAD TO LIMIT ALL YOUR WISDOM FOR YOUR CHILDREN TO ONLY TWO SHORT, SUCCINCT, AND PERFECTLY CHOSEN WORDS, WHAT WOULD THEY BE?

If you were to try and state the most profound and essential truth known to humanity in two words, how would you do it? If you had to limit all of your wisdom for your children to only two short, succinct, and perfectly chosen words, what would they be?

Let me suggest that you could never do better than *God saves.* We know the rest already: *I fail.* Yet the most important lesson we could ever learn is that *God saves.* Our heavenly Father was very deliberate when he designated that message as the name for his only begotten Son. It is as if he wanted to be absolutely sure that no one missed the point.

So let us ask the question again: What's in a name? Perhaps we should revise our earlier conclusion, for now we must agree that a wealth of meaning lies in the simple name of Jesus.

There is meaning in the fact that God chose a name of past significance. Joshua was the one who led the children of Israel into their Land of Promise, their essential legacy, after many years of slavery, grief, and rootless wandering. He brought them across the river Jordan, a barrier that had seemed insurmountable. (Jesus would be baptized in that same river before leading his children—every one of us—to our own land of promise, our own spiritual legacy.) We discover what it means to carry on our own lives of slavery to our failure, of grief, and of rootless wandering. We begin to believe we can never burst through that barrier that keeps us away from joy and peace and all that life should hold. Then the New Joshua comes along to say, "Follow me; I come that you might have life, and have it more abundantly" (John 10:10).

There is meaning in the simple fact that God chose a *common* name. In every way, the mission of his Son was to identify with people of all kinds. People of the time looked for someone bigger than life. They expected a conqueror:

a Samson or a Solomon. They didn't expect a peasant, a village carpenter clothed in humility and servanthood: "Though he was God, he did not think of equality with God as something to cling to. Instead, he gave up his divine privileges; he took the humble position of a slave and was born as a human being. When he appeared in human form, he humbled himself in obedience to God and died a criminal's death on a cross" (Philippians 2:6-8).

JESUS OF NAZARETH, A COMMON NAME FOR AN UNCOMMON MAN.

The name of Jesus was common enough that another Jesus was slated to be executed at the time of Christ's crucifixion. His name was Jesus Barabbas, and he was a terrorist and a murderer—a man who exemplified the lowest levels to which humanity could sink. It was this Jesus who was set free from the cross instead of the one who led the only perfect life in human history. Jesus of Nazareth, a common name for an uncommon man, the name of one who died so that even a murderer might have a Savior.

There is meaning in the name of Jesus now and for eternity. Jesus himself promised us that whatever we might ask in his name would be granted. We are baptized in the name of Jesus. We serve our friends and our neighbors in the name of Jesus. "There is salvation in no one else! God has given no other name under heaven by which we must be saved" (Acts 4:12). Though the time may come when life becomes difficult, when there seems to be no hope, and when everyone we know turns away from us, we draw courage and power and new strength simply from the name of Jesus.

Indeed there's something about that name. Late at night, I've been known to sit with a shortwave radio and scan the skies for the transmissions of missionary broadcasts that come from far away. Amid the aggressive static, the cacophony of voices, and the ghostly fading in and out of unknown signals, it is the music that always draws me. I recognize the unique melody of some group of believers somewhere across the world, worshiping God in music. I need not even understand the language; the harmonious joy suggests to me that Jesus lies at the heart of song and singer.

Then, whether the tongue is Swahili or Swedish, I hear the name that tends to sound the same, and to retain its beauty, in any language the human tongue might speak. At the name of Jesus the static seems to fade before my ears. At the name of Jesus I feel new delight, and I turn up the volume. Because of that one name, that one simple word, language no longer seems to be a barrier. Across the globe and the miles and the lifestyles, we share music and love and the salvation that only Jesus himself can provide.

The name of Jesus. Easy enough for a small child to say; simple enough to be the last, hopeful word upon dying lips; powerful enough to bring us through any storm, through all the intervening years. *Jesus*, "God saves," is the greatest and most powerful word humanity has ever known, and it is the final word that will be spoken when this earth and its history are finally closed, and when you and I gather together in a better place.

God elevated him to the place of highest honor
and gave him the name above all other names,
that at the name of Jesus every knee should bow,
in heaven and on earth and under the earth,
and every tongue confess that Jesus Christ is
Lord, to the glory of God the Father.

Philippians 2:9-11

What's in a name? Many things, in this case. Hope is in that name. So are power and authority, courage and consolation. And yes, there is unity. For together we will join hands and bow knees upon that day—every one of us—and pay homage to the greatest name in heaven or on earth.

Discussion Questions

◖ What is the origin of your name?

◖ Is it important to you to have a good name? Why or why not?

For further study: Read Proverbs 22:1 and Ecclesiastes 7:1. What does the Bible say about a good name?

WHY WAS JESUS BORN OF A VIRGIN?

*I*magine that moment when Joseph and Mary saw the Child for the first time. They knew this child was like no other: Angels had announced him, and prophecies had foretold him. No baby had ever been conceived in this way. As they awaited his birth, they probably wondered what the Son of God would actually look like. But could they have realized just how singular this birth was in the history of the world? Could they take in the awesome miracle of how the Son of God made his divine entrance? Can we?

The Child arrived by way of the Virgin Birth, a miraculous route to be used this time and this time only—not that the wondrous creation of life itself was anything new. In other times God had brought forth his children in a variety of different ways. He created Adam without the channel of father or mother; he made Eve from man alone; he sent Cain, Abel, and most of the rest of us through natural human reproduction; and he even used miraculous generation to bring children to elderly and barren women like Sarah in the Old Testament and Elizabeth in the New.

But the birth of Jesus was something unique and something urgently necessary. He was born of a virgin, generated completely through the miraculous work of the Holy Spirit, using Mary as his vessel to accomplish God's eternal plan. Why did God choose to make use of a virgin birth rather than, say, the way he created Adam, or even the way John the Baptist was born to Elizabeth and Zechariah?

The answer centers on the identity and mission of Jesus Christ. Even though Jesus lived among us as a fully human individual, he was also fully divine—a pre-existing, eternal person. Human parents are temporal and finite and they can pass on only limiting characteristics. "He existed in the beginning with God" (John 1:2). He has always existed, and he always will. Therefore, as Oswald Chambers has pointed out, Jesus was born *into* this world, not *from* it. He is in no way a product of the natural earth or the union of a human father and mother. Instead, he is the eternal person of the Lord himself, the infinite one who created the universe, taking on the limited form of a human being.

Among the genetic inheritances that would have come from two human parents is the imperfection that is part of the human condition. Another word for that is *sin*. As Christians, we believe that we are fallen creatures. That means that we come into this world with a capacity for corruption built into us.

If Jesus had entered the world through natural human reproduction, he would have simply been one more child of this fallen world. Therefore, God had to send him by an alternate route. Gabriel's message told Mary that Jesus would be superhuman. He would be holy at his birth—not become holy through his actions and choices—and he would be called the Son of God. Jesus had to come into the world as a full-fledged human being. However, in no way as a "reproduction" of two human parents could he not have inherited a sin nature.

Among humans, we know, a virgin birth is impossible—though with God, all things are possible. When Mary was told she would have a baby, the first question that came to her mind was the obvious one:

> *Mary asked the angel, "But how can this happen? I am a virgin."*
> *The angel replied, "The Holy Spirit will come upon you, and the power of the Most High will overshadow you. So the baby to be born will be holy, and he will be called the Son of God."*
> *Luke 1:34-35*

Mary was a simple Galilean maiden, but she knew that virgins didn't have babies.

The key word in that passage is *overshadow*. The idea in the original language is that of a great cloud enveloping someone. The people of Israel had always used that metaphor to understand God's mysterious and undeniable presence. With all his creative energy, the Lord would surround Mary with his presence and she would miraculously become pregnant. The Holy Spirit was the love knot that brought our Savior's two natures together—deity and humanity—united forever in one person. The Holy Spirit produced the Holy One within the secret place of Mary's womb. Jesus would enter it pure and perfect, from the sinless realm of eternity.

Even beyond the necessity of Jesus' having no sin within him, there are other reasons he was born of a virgin. God's eternal plan was for Jesus to come to die—to give his life as a sacrifice for all those sins, all that corruption, all that rebellion and failure that characterize our human world. Only someone *perfect* would be able to offer his life as a sacrifice; any other life would be just another human one. God alone is holy. God alone could atone for man's sin with the death of his own Son.

IF JESUS HAD ENTERED THE WORLD THROUGH NATURAL HUMAN REPRODUCTION, HE WOULD HAVE SIMPLY BEEN ONE MORE CHILD OF THIS FALLEN WORLD.

On the other hand, God is a spirit—and a spirit *cannot* die. What was the only possible solution? God must become a man, but he must retain his purity and perfection. And how could he do those two things simultaneously, when all men are sinful? Only through the miracle of the Virgin Birth. He would be divinely conceived and born, retain his perfection, but be human in every sense of the word. As a matter of fact, he would be subject to the temptations we all experience. Only if he then withstood every temptation would he be able to bring that perfect life, that worthy sacrifice, to the altar of Golgotha, the place of the cross, to exchange for our freedom.

The miracle of his conception is a fitting bookend to the miracle of his resurrection. We see in Christ someone who was fully human in every sense, yet someone who arrived and departed from this earth in ways that showed he was the Lord of nature and not its servant. He came through the miracle of the Virgin Birth; he left through the twin miracles of resurrection and ascension into heaven.

The coming of Christ is the central event of our history, the most joyful and meaningful occasion we can imagine. That's why the Virgin Birth is worthy of embracing and celebrating; the Crucifixion and Resurrection are worthy of reflection, worship, and gratitude.

The Virgin Birth also shows the master plan of God, as arranged before Creation itself. Every aspect of the holy birth was a part of his breathtakingly beautiful plan to rescue and redeem his fallen children. Here is his plan as foretold by Isaiah the prophet, who revealed so much about the nature, character, and mission of Jesus Christ:

> *The Lord himself will give you the sign. Look! The virgin will conceive a child! She will give birth to a son and will call him Immanuel (which means "God is with us").*   Isaiah 7:14

How wonderful are those four words: *God is with us.* When God is with us, the infinite has come to dwell among the finite, the perfect among the imperfect, and the world is graced by the presence of one who can never be limited by it, because it is no more than his own creation.

Finally, the Virgin Birth is a miracle. Miracles are

God's way of commanding our attention. They help people understand a truth that they won't see otherwise. Jesus said about his miracles, "They prove that [the Father] sent me" (John 5:36). What does his miraculous birth testify?

It tells us first of all that with God, all things are possible. From the very moment of the angel's annunciation, the message was clear: Mighty things will occur through the life and person of Jesus Christ. The Virgin Birth was like a great trumpet blast from heaven, heralding the approach of a king. Yes, that king would be an infant. But he would be like no other infant ever born because his origin would be "from the distant past" (Micah 5:2).

It tells us that everything about Jesus was pure and holy. There could never be any possibility that he might have inherited a bad temper. He lived his entire life without the sin or the rebellion that stains all other human beings.

> THERE MUST BE A NATIVITY IN EVERY HUMAN HEART, THE PERFECT COMING TO DWELL WITHIN THE IMPERFECT; FOR WE CANNOT GIVE BIRTH TO HIM, OR TO HIS GOODNESS, ON OUR OWN EFFORTS.

The Hebrew idea of holiness was "set apart." Jesus was set apart from conception in a way that no other person could possibly be. Some have suggested that the Holy Spirit overshadowed Mary all through her pregnancy, separating the baby from any effects of sin. By comparison, Mary's relative Elizabeth became pregnant in a miracle of her own, at almost the same time. Yet though God intervened in her pregnancy, too, it was not a virgin birth. John the Baptist had two biological parents and no divinity in his origin.

As we contemplate all these things, we realize the miracle that must occur for each of us who would follow Jesus. Just as he was born into this world and not from it, he must be born into our lives the same way. Christ does not naturally live in any believer; he must invade that believer from outside, just as he invaded the world. There must be a Nativity in every human heart, the perfect coming to dwell within the imperfect; for we cannot give birth to him, or to his goodness, on our own efforts.

We are flawed but he is holy. We need him to miraculously enter our lives, still and quiet as he did on that Bethlehem morning. We need to know what it means to be clean. We need to know what it is to have fellowship with God. Only if he lives again on this earth through our lives, in all his perfection and purity, working through our humanity and opportunity, will we ever know how wonderful it is that the Son of God could be born of a virgin, yet love us in our imperfections.

Discussion Questions

◌ Which of the five ways that God used for creating people seems the most amazing to you? Why?

◌ Do you agree with the statement, "The coming of Christ is the central event in our history"? Why or why not?

For further study: Read Colossians 1:15-17 and Hebrews 1:1-3. How do these passages support the necessity of the Virgin Birth?

WHY DID JESUS COME AS A BABY?

In those first speechless moments, new parents gaze with fascination. They lovingly examine every inch of their newborn child's face.

No matter how we prepare ourselves, the reality of new birth astounds us. Here, nestled in our arms, is a brand-new member of the human race. Here is the future in flesh; our legacy to the world. We check eyes, mouth, ears for telltale family resemblances; we marvel at the delicate dewy skin. Most of all, we silently thank the Lord over and over for a gift so unimaginably wonderful.

Can you imagine how intently Joseph and Mary must have studied the Child who came to them in Bethlehem? His coming had been foretold not by physicians but by angels. If those angels were right—and how could they not be?—here in the starlight was a Messiah who had been the subject of poems, songs, and dreams for a thousand years.

Messiah: Perhaps the couple stammered when they tried to speak the *M*-word aloud. It was just so hard to imagine such a magnificent personification when they looked at the sleeping infant.

After all, everyone knew (or thought they knew) that the Messiah would be the ultimate military commander. He would arrive on horseback, with sword held high, crying out for vengeance and redemption in the name of the Lord and his favored nation. The Chosen One would have the wisdom of Solomon, the charisma of David, the godliness of Moses, and the military genius of Joshua.

Yet here was a baby—just a baby. Joseph and Mary had to admit that here was a baby who seemed, at first glance, like any other newborn child. He cried in the middle of the night. He hungered for milk. He needed fresh "swaddling clothes" every now and then. If this was just an ordinary child like cousin Elizabeth's new addition, how could he be "one whose origins are from the deep past," as the prophet had insisted? How could an infant be the Son of God?

Or for that matter, why would the Son of God be an infant? The need of crumbling, dying Israel was urgent. First the Greek and now the Roman influence was wiping away a bit more of the legacy of Abraham, Isaac, and Jacob each day.

Why, indeed? Why did Jesus come as a child?

Jesus is the one like no other, for he was fully human and fully divine—simultaneously. Nothing about his humanity could detract from his godliness; nothing about his godliness could detract from his humanity. Only because this is true can he reconcile the Father in heaven with his children on earth. He is the Man of both worlds;

he is the bridge by which God comes to earth and people come to heaven.

In that regard, we have seen that the Virgin Birth is the sign of his *divinity*. He comes to the earth from outside, pure and clean, and he is in no way a product of this world. Now we see that, in the same way, the infancy of the Child is the sign of his *humanity*. He is one of us in every way. He arrives from heaven with perfection and godliness of which no man or woman is capable—yet he takes the full human journey, which even God in heaven had not taken. How could we follow his footsteps as a man if we hadn't seen him crawl as a child? How could we believe he had undergone all the temptation we have faced if he had bypassed the most difficult years in which we struggle to earn our adulthood?

To make the full sacrifice on our behalf, Jesus had to make the full commitment. It would have meant very little to us if he had sprung from heaven fully formed, bathed in heavenly glory, saying, "Here are my hands and my feet—place me upon the cross, for I am willing to die."

HOW COULD WE FOLLOW HIS FOOTSTEPS AS A MAN IF WE HADN'T SEEN HIM CRAWL AS A CHILD?

Instead, we see him as a child in a manger. We see him at the Temple as a boy on the verge of maturity, already about his Father's business. We see Mary and Joseph wondering at him, trying to understand, as he grew "in wisdom and in stature and in favor with God and all the people" (Luke 2:52).

Finally, we see him as a young man, quietly beginning a

ministry that will change all of human history. We overhear the whispers from his neighbors: "He's just a carpenter's son, and we know Mary, his mother, and his brothers—James, Joseph, Simon, and Judas. All his sisters live right here among us" (Matthew 13:55-56).

We see him in the desert, wrestling with temptation and the matter of his destiny, and we know he is fully human. We see his love for children, and we can believe it because he, too, has been a child. And then, when those crude spikes are drilled through his wrists and his ankles, we know he feels the pain that any man would feel. We know the price of our sins is on the table, being paid in full with no credit plans or easy payment schedules, but by every last drop of blood and every brutal slash of the whip. We are bought with a price that could never have been paid without the full burden of humanity having been accepted.

If he had been God only, his sacrifice would have been cheap and unconvincing. If he had been man only, his sacrifice would have had no power; he would have been a martyr like ten thousand others.

But he was man and he was God, and therefore he was all in all. He came as a child to confront and conquer every challenge and every temptation common to humanity. We trust him with our lives because he was God. We love him with our hearts because we know that once he was a tiny baby, wrapped in swaddling clothes, lying in a manger.

Discussion Questions

- Why are most of us fascinated with a newborn baby?
- Does it seem important to you that Jesus lived life on earth as a human? Why or why not?

For further study: Read Hebrews 2:16-18. How can we take comfort from Jesus' coming as a baby?

WHY THE SHEPHERDS?

𝓗ow prestigious was a local shepherd at the time of Jesus' birth? One line in the book of Genesis tells us all we need to know about shepherds' social standing.

Joseph, an Israelite who had risen to a seat of power in Egypt, was giving his brothers advice on how to be accepted. Foreigners were not always welcome. Joseph's advice was for the brothers to admit to the Pharaoh that they had been livestock breeders for many generations. "When Pharaoh calls for you and asks you about your occupation," said Joseph, "he will let you live here in the region of Goshen, for the Egyptians despise shepherds" (Genesis 46:33-34).

As a matter of fact, they were despised elsewhere, as well. Sheepherding was one of those occupations that everyone needed and no one desired. Hebrews in particular prized cleanliness and purity. Life among sheep lent itself to tired feet, long work shifts, and unwanted aromas. Bears and lions roamed the wilderness. The sheep tended to wander, and the shepherd was expected to seek the lost among the treacherous cliffs. And of course, no other job could have been quite so lonely. No wonder David, a shepherd boy whom God fashioned into a king, turned his creative mind toward poetry and song. A shepherd needed to pass the long hours in some way or another.

That suggests a compelling thought. In David, God made a shepherd into a king; in Jesus, he made a king into a sacrificial lamb. Thus our Lord is eternally confounding the equations we create for the purpose of operating this world and its customs. He chose Bethlehem, not Rome or Athens or even Jerusalem. He chose Israel, a downtrodden country that had nearly forgotten its birthright. And he chose peasants for parents.

Then, when the blessed event occurred on that night in Bethlehem, who received invitations to greet the newborn king? The world's emperors? Priests and prophets? Soldiers and scholars?

Yes, it's true that the wise men came from a distant land, and they bore precious gifts of gold, frankincense, and myrrh. It is also true that heaven itself broke forth in a choir of angels, praising God in the night sky. But who were the first human visitors? That was an honor reserved for the lowliest of the low, the least educated of men, ranch hands who were despised by the local gentry. Men whose skin glistened with sweat, whose clothes gave off the stench of the fields; those who lacked the most basic manners, who used language unfit for your children's ears; minimum-wage earners who were unlikely to be admitted to any respectable establishment of the time—on this night they were favored by heaven.

They bore names nowhere recorded in the Bible. Yet whatever their names may have been, they graced the guest list for the most joyful moment human history had yet contained.

It is the wise men who are the favorites of Christmas-card artists, of painters through the ages. Our eyes enjoy their rich finery and exotic pomp. Our minds are captivated by the long journey they took, following a star. The expensive gifts are exactly what we would expect and what any king would deserve. Who, after all, should attend a royal coronation but foreign dignitaries bearing rich gifts? Wise men, not ignorant ones.

Yet, as if to set the tone for the entire life and message of his Son, God brought a delegation of shepherds to be the first to see, to worship, to celebrate. He invited simple men to take the low road and wise men to take the high road, because from that moment, all roads would lead to the manger and the Child.

He was only a few moments or a few hours old, but Jesus would have liked that. This was the one who would enter the homes of despised tax collectors and known sinners when he came of age three decades hence. This teacher, with so little time allotted him to minister on earth—no more than three years—always had time for the pressing crowds. He touched lepers—with his fingers and with his love. He spoke of the greatness of servanthood, of the first being the last. He said that for anyone who served the "least of these," it would be counted as if they served Jesus himself.

The Child of the Nativity would become a man who rebuked his disciples for dismissing little children. "Let them come unto me," he would say—just as his Father had one day said, "Let these shepherds come."

Imagine the wonder of that evening for those humble field hands. One moment the skies were dark, and their moods were perhaps darker. The next moment angels were in their presence—angels with amazing news. Surely the shepherds shared our questions: "Why here? Why us?" And they were afraid.

But these simple men followed the simple instructions the angels had given them. They made their way to Bethlehem and took part in an experience that countless generations of Christians have envied. As they left, they told everyone in their path of the things that had happened to them. Their lives would never again be the same; the sky would never seem so dark. They would know that just as they kept watch over their sheep by night, Someone far greater was keeping watch over them.

GOD INVITED SIMPLE MEN TO TAKE THE LOW ROAD AND WISE MEN TO TAKE THE HIGH ROAD, BECAUSE FROM THAT MOMENT, ALL ROADS WOULD LEAD TO THE MANGER AND THE CHILD.

And perhaps as they grew old, their minds returned to that remarkable picture of the skies opening up. As soon as the first angel had delivered his message, "a vast host of others—the armies of heaven" (Luke 2:13) appeared, all of them praising God: "Glory to God in highest heaven, and peace on earth to those with whom God is pleased" (Luke 2:14).

These words would not be forgotten—not as long as the shepherds had life and breath. Angels could appear to them. To *them*. And there would be peace on earth "to those with whom God is pleased."

And who would have thought that God might favor a shepherd?

Discussion Questions

◌ Who would be the equivalent of shepherds in society today? Why?

◌ How do you respond to these people when they intersect your daily life? What could you do to improve that?

For further study: Read John 10:1-11. What other reason might there be for Jesus' birth being announced first to the shepherds?

WHY THE ANGELS?

$\mathcal{F}$amilies all over the world enjoy decorating their homes with Nativity sets made of wood, ceramic, or stone. The scene is a beloved one to us, and we enjoy lingering over each of the elements and its meaning.

At the very center, of course, are Mary, Joseph, and the baby Jesus in his manger. The animals share their gentle presence. Entering the stable tentatively, worshipfully, come the shepherds. And just behind them (though we know they arrived later) we place the wise men in their colorful garb, bearing their gifts. The camels add visual interest and bring a smile to our faces.

But what about the angels? They add ethereal beauty and grace to the tableau, but we're never certain where to place them. After all, they should be in the "sky" above our Nativity set, shouldn't they?

We tend to place the angels on the periphery of the scene, almost at a distance. In truth, however, the angels cannot be an afterthought. As the Bible demonstrates, they occupy the very center of this spectacular story. What is their role in the great event, and what is the nature of these mysterious heavenly agents?

You may visualize angels in white robes with wide, feathery wings. Perhaps you even picture shiny gold halos. This image comes not from the Bible but from painters of the Middle Ages and Renaissance. These artists were disappointed to discover that the Bible is largely silent about the physical appearance of angels. How to describe the indescribable? The artists had to substitute their own creativity.

We can know this about the appearance of angels: If we saw one, we would most likely be terrified. As we find in the New Testament, the first words from an angel's mouth are usually, "Don't be afraid!" People weren't used to seeing them, but as the birth of Christ approached, angelic activity picked up considerably in the land of Judea. Consider these recipients of angelic visits:

Zechariah, who would be the father of John the Baptist;

Mary, learning that the Son of God would be born to her;

Joseph, being reassured to support Mary and take her as his wife; and

The shepherds, urged to hurry to Bethlehem and worship the King.

And don't forget the wise men! Where was their angel? We are told that they were "warned in a dream" that Herod, the king, was treacherous and should be avoided. Perhaps it was an angel who spoke in that dream, as in the dream of Joseph. Who can explain the business of the angels? They come in dreams or in real time; they appear in a fearsome display, or they come disguised as ordinary people. (Hebrews 13:2 tells us that in showing hospitality, many have "entertained angels without realizing it"!)

What matters is that angels are busy carrying out the urgent work of God. Most often, they bring messages of critical importance to God's people. But they perform other tasks as well: ministering to Jesus in the wilderness or in the garden of Gethsemane, rolling away the stone of his tomb, even assisting Peter in a prison escape! (See Acts 12:6-10.)

The angel who spoke to Zechariah was comforting, as usual, but also an agent of discipline: When Zechariah doubted, the angel struck him speechless until his son was born. That son, John the Baptist, would play such an important role in the life of Jesus that his birth, too, needed to be heralded by a miracle and an angel.

It was the same messenger, Gabriel, who visited Mary—one of those special angels we know by name. For his part, Joseph encountered his visitor in a dream, but the message was just as important. Mary needed the support that her husband could bring. In each case, the angels gave careful instruction, which Mary and Joseph followed. Why angels? Because we are not likely to ignore the advice of such spectacular guests.

Then there were the shepherds. How touching that society's least appreciated workers would have their own angelic experience. What does this tell us about God? He sent angels for very practical reasons to Mary and Joseph. But the shepherds? We can only conclude that God is loving and full of surprises. He wanted humble peasants to attend the birth, even though they would play no other part in the life of Jesus.

NO HOLIDAY FIREWORKS COULD POSSIBLY MEASURE UP TO THIS SPECTACLE. AND NOTHING COULD HAVE BEEN MORE UNEXPECTED.

It is worth noting that the shepherds enjoyed the most elaborate of the angelic visits. First, there was the usual single angel—the message bearer. He soothed the shepherds' fear, invited them to Bethlehem, and gave specific instructions on how to find the family of Jesus. But then, "Suddenly, the angel was joined by a vast host of others—the armies of heaven—praising God and saying, 'Glory to God in highest heaven, and peace on earth to those with whom God is pleased'" (Luke 2:13-14).

This was a sky show such as the world has never seen. No holiday fireworks could possibly measure up to this spectacle. And nothing could have been more unexpected. There was no practical "task" orientation about this incredible display by the armies of heaven, presented to the senses of the least-important citizens of the province. This was a spontaneous outpouring of joy! This was a moment of heartfelt worship that began in heaven and broke through into our world. In this moment, when lowly shepherds were invited to the presence of God's Son, what other response could there be but joy and praise among the servants of God?

When it was over, we are told that the angels "returned to heaven." But thankfully, not for good. They would come again, and many times.

Surely there are angels at work even this moment—perhaps in your life. We may not see them, but we can surely follow their lead. How? By staying busy with the work of heaven; by telling people that God is moving; and—every now and then—by exploding in the simple joy of seeing the miracle that is Christ alive in our world.

Discussion Questions

ᗏ How do you think you would respond if an angel of God appeared and spoke to you? Why?

ᗏ Which of the various angelic visits in this chapter is the most meaningful to you? Why?

For further study: Read Hebrews 2:5-9. What do we learn about Jesus and angels in this passage? What does it mean to you?

WHY THE
WISE MEN?

*T*here is something magical and mysterious about the age-old picture. From across a continent, over the desert sand, beneath the silent stars trudges a curious caravan. In distant lands, these men have read signs and portents in the evening sky, sensing an incredible truth that few other living souls were to recognize for many years.

We remember them as the wise men, or (using the Gospel's name) the *magi*. From that word we derive *magic*, and it is indeed a story filled with wonder.

Just who were these visitors from the East? What were they seeking, and how did they find their hearts' desire? Why was such a precious invitation given to them?

Paintings and pageants can't seem to agree. We see the magi as monarchs or magicians, ambassadors or astrologers—three kings or three wise men? We like to envision them in colorful and exotic attire, preferably with camels.

For centuries we have speculated about their identity. Not all the answers are available to us, but perhaps there is just enough light to guide our quest for the wise men of history. Like the magi themselves, perhaps we can follow that light toward the answers we seek.

They were first sighted in the vicinity of Jerusalem, asking questions. "Where is the newborn king of the Jews?" they inquired. "We saw his star as it rose, and we have come to worship him" (Matthew 2:2).

Out-of-towners were by no means uncommon in Jerusalem. The local folk would have recognized these particular visitors as coming from some Eastern land—probably Persia or Arabia. Their interest in stars would have marked them as astrologers: readers of the skies. There had been a time when many of Israel's people had been held in captivity in these distant lands, and the science of the stars would have been familiar to them.

Yet these visitors had come to Judea—such a long and treacherous journey—to follow one point of light in the sky. This was something new. So the magi were given a careful explanation of just where the newborn king would be found: *Bethlehem*. The prophet Micah had linked that town and its future significance long ago (see Micah 5:2).

Matthew tells us that the star appeared once again, to the magi's delight. It led them indeed to the little town of Bethlehem, where they found the unassuming family they sought. We have seen many colorful pictures of the scene that followed. But are the pictures correct?

Painters through the ages have enjoyed showing the elegant wise men worshiping a newborn Jesus, whose family was too poor for a room, on Christmas night. We imagine the visitors arriving just behind the shepherds. But such an idea never came from the Bible.

Matthew tells us that when the magi arrived, the scene was not the rustic birthplace of Christmas evening, but a *house* (see Matthew 2:11). It would seem that a few weeks or even months had passed, and by this time, Joseph and Mary had situated their little family in a more suitable home.

Therefore, it was a bit later that the three of them came—or was it three? As a matter of fact, three names have traditionally been associated with the wise men: Balthasar, Melchior, and Caspar. But it's only since the seventh century that these names have been attached to the mysterious visitors. We can't be certain of names or number. However, we do know the names and number of the gifts, and indeed they were three—gold, frankincense, and myrrh. Perhaps there were three presenters for the three presents.

Thus, just as surely as the shepherds took the "low road" to the baby Jesus, we have the magi, who took the "high road." One group came from the immediate vicinity; one from a great distance. One group came from practical peasantry; one from a setting of wealth and wisdom. One came on that unforgettable night; one arrived sometime later. They came by different roads and left with united hearts. The shepherds returned to their flocks, joyfully praising God (see Luke 2:20). But the wise men went "to their own country by another route" (Matthew 2:12) after yet another sign: a dream that told them King Herod represented a threat to their lives.

And there, on that highway vanishing into the East, we

lose sight of the wise men again. Mysteriously they appeared, and mysteriously they are gone. We are left with so many questions about them. How were their lives changed? What did they tell friends in their homeland? What became of those remarkable gifts?

Plays and pageants and pictures have offered imaginary answers. But the better questions—those posed by our hearts—are clearly answered in Matthew's brief sketch of the magi.

For example, there is the question, *Who might seek the Lord of lords?* We see, with great joy, that shepherds and sheikhs alike are invited to come—rich and poor, neighbor and newcomer.

THE MAGI
WENT HOME
BY ANOTHER
WAY; SO DO WE.
IN THE PRESENCE
OF CHRIST, ALL
ROADS BECOME
NEW TO US.

We ask, *How can we find the way?* The magi followed the heavens and their hearts. The glories of God are written in the very skies; his voice calls to us from within. The wise men followed the light of a star, and God accommodated the limited wisdom of their time and place. How much greater is the wisdom available to us? God still invites us, and his invitation is written wherever our eyes may linger.

What gifts can we bring him? The magi teach us that the answer is, Whatever we find in our hands. The visitors brought the gifts most logical to them, those that might be presented to any emperor. Yet the shepherds brought only their delight and their praise.

Where will we go now? The magi went home by another way; so do we. In the presence of Christ, all roads become new to us; all roads lead to the home that the Child has prepared for us. And whatever gifts we may have brought are obscured in the brilliance of the Gift that has become our own.

We would be wise men and women, too. Therefore, we follow in their path, seeking the wonder of a newborn king:

> *O star of wonder, star of night,*
> *Star with royal beauty bright,*
> *Westward leading, still proceeding,*
> *Guide us to thy perfect light.*

Discussion Questions

◌ How do you go about selecting gifts for people, especially at Christmastime? What motivates you to do it this way?

◌ The others in the Nativity story who had visits from angels were Jewish, while the wise men were Gentiles. Why do you think the wise men obeyed the angels' warning?

For further study: Read Isaiah 60:1-3 and Acts 26:22-23. What do we learn from these passages about the promises of God to the Gentiles?

WHY THE STAR OF BETHLEHEM?

Star of wonder. Star of night.

The sky is filled with stars. In the pure air of ancient times, you could see them sparkling from horizon to horizon. But one evening there appeared a star of special distinction. It shines forever in our hearts as the star of Bethlehem.

What was it about that single point of light in the West Asian firmament? What compelled the magi to put aside all they were doing to undertake a long and dangerous journey, following one shimmering star across the landscape?

Angels and shepherds are one matter, but a star—that enlarges the borders of our discussion, doesn't it? For now we have entered the realm of science. Stars are the special province of astronomers, who can give us all the facts and figures. Scientists might be quick to tell us that stars don't "move," relatively speaking; that they surely don't linger above particular towns; and that they are governed by the laws of physics rather than those of faith.

SCIENTISTS MIGHT BE QUICK TO TELL US THAT STARS DON'T "MOVE," THAT THEY SURELY DON'T LINGER ABOVE PARTICULAR TOWNS, AND THAT THEY ARE GOVERNED BY THE LAWS OF PHYSICS RATHER THAN THOSE OF FAITH.

But science tells only a small part of any story. "In our world," says a child in one of the Narnia tales, "a star is a huge ball of flaming gas." His wiser friend replies, "Even in your world, my son, that is not what a star is, but only what it is made of."

So there is more to this celestial body than its vital statistics. What can we know about the star of Bethlehem?

For one thing, it shines only in the second chapter of Matthew; it makes no other biblical appearances. The scene is Jerusalem. Our friends the wise men are seen there one day, asking questions concerning Jewish political affairs. The visitors themselves, of course, are non-Jews. They have brought their question to Jerusalem because they know it to be the religious and political capital of Judea.

"Where is the newborn king of the Jews?" ask the Eastern visitors. "We saw his star as it rose, and we have come to worship him" (Matthew 2:2). The question surely raises many eyebrows in a Roman-occupied city in the hustle and bustle of daily business. Jewish king? Such an idea is nearly laughable in the presence of Caesar's armies. Perhaps these tourists have arrived several centuries too late.

Yet the wise men adopt a more cosmic view. They are astrologers, seeking to understand human events by reading the constellations. It is their habit to compare the skies to prophetic literature, including the Jewish scriptures. Those scrolls speak of a "King of the Jews" whose coming will be heralded by a star.

The magi possess a copy of those scrolls. Among the most ancient of the writings is found this tantalizing reference:

> *I see him, but not here and now.*
> *I perceive him, but far in the distant future.*
> *A star will rise from Jacob;*
> *a scepter will emerge from Israel.*
>
> *Numbers 24:17*

In those days, those who trafficked in classical prophecies knew that stars and kings were intertwined by destiny. A scepter was a symbol of royalty. So for the wise men, there was nothing ambiguous about these words. They called for a great king, announced with the silent fanfare of a brilliant light. And if such a king was foretold more than one thousand years earlier, he was worth traveling to see.

That explains the prophecy. But again, why this particular star in a sky filled with them? We have wondered for centuries. Modern science promotes a number of candidates for the special light that the wise men saw. Halley's Comet, for example, made a visit during that era. Jupiter and Saturn were aligned to create a bright "star" in 7 BC.

Jupiter was seen as carrying a special royal status. Another theory concerns the fact that the constellation Aries was associated with Judea and the lands ruled by Herod—and that Jupiter and the moon were aligned in a brilliant evening display in spring of 6 BC.

Is it possible, then, that the wise men got themselves excited over a perfectly ordinary astronomical event? If so, does that invalidate the importance of the star of Bethlehem? Not at all! Remember the wise words from Narnia: A star is more than a ball of flaming gas. The constellations are governed not only by the laws of physics but by the one who oversees those laws at every moment. The star may have been a light that appeared for one brief, shining moment in the skies of Matthew 2. It may have been a special incarnation of lights and planets that we still enjoy. It may even have been one more angel—a messenger from God inviting visitors from a distant land to see the Nativity. Whatever it was, it led the magi directly to the presence of the Christ child, where they worshiped and presented their gifts.

Perhaps the solution to the star is more wonderful for us as an unsolved mystery; a Christmas gift not to be unwrapped until that eternal day when night skies are no more, and when all our questions will be answered. What matters so much more is the *meaning* of the star, for its light breaks through the pages of the gospel, calling us to come and worship. It is still a star of wonder. It is still a star of night that captivates us with its silent beauty and the wonderful announcement that it brings with a twinkle.

We love the star of Bethlehem because it shines bright enough that people of other faiths and other lands might join us at the manger. It shone for Jews, Greeks, Romans, Arabians, and anyone else who might look to Bethlehem. It dominated the night sky, reminding us that our faith is great enough for the world to enjoy.

This star, *our* star, broke through the galaxies to remind us that the intimate story of the Nativity—as close and warm as mother and child—is written on the widest of canvases. The tiny Child is the Lord of Creation. The star leads us to the light of his presence. And once we are there, even a star seems dim by comparison.

Discussion Questions

◌ Do you place a star or an angel atop your Christmas tree? Why?

◌ Do you think it was faith or science that caused the magi to follow the star? Why?

For further study: When the wise men saw the star (see Matthew 2:10), they rejoiced greatly. Read Exodus 18:9, 1 Kings 5:7, and Acts 16:25-34 to find more examples of Gentiles rejoicing at the work of God. List each example and tell why the people rejoiced.

WHY WAS KING HEROD
SO ANGRY?

*T*he Judean province where Jesus was born lay beneath a double curse.

The primary burden, of course, was its occupation by the Roman Empire. In 63 BC, Pompey, the Roman general, stormed Jerusalem and claimed the entire region for Rome. For years there had been several factions squabbling over ownership of Jerusalem; now the Romans were in firm control.

The second shadow was cast by Herod, king of the Jews. His is a familiar name in the Nativity story. Who exactly was Herod—and what part did he play in the coming of Christ?

He was the son of Antipater, who had been appointed procurator of Judea when the Romans ascended to power in the territory. But in 44 BC, Caesar was assassinated in Rome. A civil war erupted there, and when the smoke cleared, Mark Antony was one of the winners. He favored

Antipater's son Herod, a half-Jew, to keep order in Judea. The Roman Senate even named him "King of the Jews" in 37 BC, as if that would carry any weight with the common folk. It certainly didn't. Even with Roman backing, Herod had to fight for thirty-three years to secure his position.

Maintaining a far-flung empire is perilous business. As the Romans struggled to keep order at home and in many other places, Herod had to be on his guard at his own Middle Eastern outpost. Cleopatra of Egypt wanted to steal this real estate for her people. Syrian and Greek factions were active. Then, of course, there were the Jews themselves, who hated Herod. They saw him kill the high priest and many other priests. He routinely assassinated anyone who could possibly be considered disloyal to him.

So even when Herod began rebuilding the fallen Temple in a calculated move to win the hearts of the Jews, they resented him still. After all, wasn't he also building temples to all sorts of pagan gods? Wasn't he simply a tool of the Roman outsiders, whose soldiers crucified peasants simply for public intimidation? Didn't he enforce their outrageous taxes, as well as demanding his own, as the Romans allowed him to do?

Herod stood no chance of ever being a beloved ruler or of having his own people acknowledge him as king of the Jews. He would never occupy his throne without a furtive glance into the shadows of the room. He knew that with the slightest shift of political winds back in Italy, he would be ousted and probably slain. It would take only one concentrated uprising by the Jewish rebels to overcome all his security precautions.

It was not good to be king—yet Herod the Great fought to keep what he had. It's not surprising that the king suffered from paranoia, as well as an incurable physical disease. As the time approached for the birth of Christ, he was in his final days, an old man immersed in pain and bitterness. As an obscure peasant and his pregnant wife approached the town of Bethlehem for a census, King Herod was six miles away at Herodium, his proud fortress. It stood high on a hill, in sight of the City of David.

The miserable king was thinking about death at the very time when someone was coming to conquer it. He was making funeral arrangements, attempting suicide (unsuccessfully), and lying awake through the night, wondering who would come in the night to steal his crown.

THE MISERABLE KING WAS THINKING ABOUT DEATH AT THE VERY TIME WHEN SOMEONE WAS COMING TO CONQUER IT.

It was during these days of decline that the king's advisors briefed him on an interesting occurrence in the city: Visitors from the East had been asking questions in Jerusalem. They wanted to know where they might find the King of the Jews. The king, they were told, was out of town at present; he was resting at his private retreat and wished not to be disturbed.

"I beg your pardon, no," the visitors would have said. "We seek the *new* King of the Jews, whose birth was revealed to us by a star."

Herod may have heard about the commotion in

Bethlehem—some woman giving birth in a cave and shepherds worshiping the child. It could all be dismissed as crazy talk during the commotion of the Roman census. However, we are told that "all of Jerusalem" was abuzz over the quest of the wise men.

Herod took notice. If there remained in his life any purpose by this time, it was to root out heirs apparent. He had been doing so for years, and there was already blood on his hands—the blood of his own wife, his mother-in-law, his brother-in-law, three of his sons, and forty-six priests, along with untold others. In a world of poverty, he lived in the richest palace, yet we can be certain he was miserable, his heart dark, his soul ruined, his days riddled with self-loathing. By this time it would have been little more than a reflex action to order one more death . . . or a few hundred of them.

Meanwhile, a short walk away, another King of the Jews occupied the crude throne of an animal trough. His legacy was not death but life, not misery but joy, not clutching what he had but giving it away. Instead of having the blood of others on his hands, this King's blood would be freely given to buy his people's pardon. And while the throne of Herod would soon be dust, Jesus would rule forever.

Herod tried to manipulate the wise men to lead him to the child. When that failed, he decided to simply kill *all* the infant males two years old and under, to be sure he wiped the slate clean of any future competition. That plot, too, was thwarted. Herod didn't reckon upon the possibility that God, who fills thrones and topples them, might even then be working his own purposes.

Herod died soon after. You can visit the impressive ruins of Herodium and see the dust of his legacy. As for the wise men, they went home by another way.

And the little King in the manger? He rules even today, wise, good, and beloved by billions of subjects. You can visit his palace, too. It is alive and growing more beautiful each day, as children come by the thousands and the ten thousands to join his eternal kingdom of life and light.

Discussion Questions

- ᴗ It is said that people often react with anger when they are afraid. Do you agree? Why or why not?

- ᴗ Herod's name means "heroic." Do you think he was a hero? Why or why not?

For further study: Read Jeremiah 31:15 and Matthew 2:16-18. How are these two passages of Scripture related?

WHY DID THE WISE MEN BRING GIFTS?

$\mathcal{T}$he Child may have been almost two years old. His family continued to make their home in Bethlehem. The town was quiet again, and that allowed Joseph and Mary to upgrade their living conditions to a small house.

Soon the little family would be on the move once more, when an angel warned them of approaching danger. Just before that unexpected visit, however, came another one. A knock at the door revealed delegates from a faraway country. Joseph, always protective, may have been wary of these oddly dressed visitors. But their faces were kind and eager; their eyes were bright and reverent. They claimed they had traveled for many weeks, at great expense and greater risk, to see the newborn King.

The shepherds, of course, had come on the night when Jesus was born. But just as Mary and Joseph might have wondered how long their special child would remain a secret to the world, there appeared these men to affirm that

Jesus was the Christ, the Messiah. The fact that they were non-Jews and even foreigners suggested that the Child was more than a *Jewish* Messiah. As Gabriel said, he is the Son of God; therefore he belongs to the world, as the world belongs to him.

What an ornate caravan these wise men must have brought, for they wouldn't have traveled such a great distance alone. The wise men must have inspired a great deal of talk in Bethlehem, just as they had done in Jerusalem. Indeed, the couple had to depart quietly for Egypt soon afterward—and when they did, the gifts of these wise men may have financed the trip.

And what about those gifts? We don't have the names of the magi nor the number of their delegation, but we are told what they brought. Mary and Joseph were unlikely to forget the extravagant substances that were laid at the child's feet. "They entered the house and saw the child with his mother, Mary, and they bowed down and worshiped him. Then they opened their treasure chests and gave him gifts of gold, frankincense, and myrrh" (Matthew 2:11).

The object of their entire rigorous quest was one of worship, and worship of a God probably not their own. This Child was for everyone, and the gifts would reflect both the givers and the recipient.

We imagine the first visitor stepping forth and opening his small chest to reveal a breathtaking sight: *gold.* This gift needed little explanation. Throughout the world, gold was coveted as the most precious of metals; the standard by which all other wealth was measured. That's why gold is a royal gift symbolizing kingship. Only as partakers of divine revelation would these visitors from a pagan world be able to fall at the feet of an ordinary peasant child in a small village and acknowledge him as king. Their background and their long travel proved their commitment. A gift of gold demonstrated hearts of sacrifice.

John Henry Hopkins Jr. gave us the classic hymn, "We Three Kings," which includes each of the gifts in turn:

Born a King on Bethlehem's plain,
Gold I bring to crown him again,
King forever, ceasing never
Over us all to reign.

The little casket of gold was closed again and set to one side of the Child, who perhaps rested in his mother's lap, his eyes wide at the oriental spectacle. Now another visitor stepped forward, this time to open a vial. A delicious fragrance permeated the small room: the aroma of *frankincense*, the second of the gifts. This was holy oil, well familiar to anyone who lived near Jerusalem. To sniff its pungency reminded one of a visit to the Temple. As the cloud of fragrance spread, it suggested the pure and beautiful presence of God among the fellowship of believers. Its name means "whiteness" and typifies purity.

THE OBJECT OF THEIR ENTIRE RIGOROUS QUEST WAS ONE OF WORSHIP, AND WORSHIP OF A GOD PROBABLY NOT THEIR OWN.

Only priests could make an incense offering, and only to God. But in Jesus, of course, all men and women would become priests. All people could step boldly into the Lord's presence, and no Temple would be necessary. If gold was a gift that said *kingship*, frankincense said *godliness*. Joseph and Mary may have trembled at this new sensation, the aroma of the Temple in their own humble home. But it helped them remember that the presence of Jesus there should cause them to wonder even more.

> *Frankincense to offer have I;*
> *Incense owns a Deity nigh;*
> *Prayer and praising, all men raising,*
> *Worship him, God on high.*

Then came the third and final gift. As it was opened, Mary may have felt a little foreboding shudder. Some of the luxurious aroma of frankincense was now covered by the smell of myrrh. It, too, had a familiar association.

Myrrh was an anointing oil used for embalming the dead. It would be the final smell associated with a lost loved one. It was the scent of bereavement. The magi brought it because it, too, was a precious oil for anointing, and a gift valued in any land. David had been anointed with it by Samuel. But its aroma was slightly bitter, and for the common Judean, it was the very smell of death.

The day would come when Jesus would be offered this gift again, but on this later occasion he would refuse it. "They brought Jesus to a place called Golgotha (which means 'Place of the Skull'). They offered him wine drugged with myrrh, but he refused it. Then the soldiers nailed him to the cross" (Mark 15:22-24).

Myrrh is mine. Its bitter perfume
Breathes a life of gathering gloom:
Sorrowing, sighing, bleeding, dying,
Sealed in the stone-cold tomb.

After the gifts were given, we are told, the magi went home by another way for the purpose of safety. The Child would go home by another way, too. But he would choose the most terrible of routes. He made a gift of himself to all of us, then returned home to his Father. That gift was far more precious than gold or any other substance. As our King, our God, and our sacrificial Lamb, he gave us all he had.

Discussion Questions

ⵀ Which of the gifts of the wise men would you most like to receive? Why?

ⵀ If you were able to give Jesus a material gift today, what would you bring? Why?

For further study: The only writers of the Bible who included a record of Jesus' birth, Matthew and Luke, also included other similar incidents in their Gospels, although, as with their birth accounts, there are slight differences. Read Matthew 7:11 and Luke 11:13. How are they alike? How are they different?

WHY DIDN'T JESUS HAVE A ROYAL BIRTH?

$\mathcal{A}$fter seeing the great star in the sky, the wise men traveled to Jerusalem. As educated men, they knew that this was the most logical place to find a Hebrew king.

After all, Jerusalem had been Israel's capital city in the glory days; it was the dwelling place of royalty. The town was set high in the hills, as if it presided over the landscape from its natural throne.

In the earliest days of this nation, just after their Promised Land was settled, the people of Israel had looked directly to God for leadership. They followed his spokesmen and leaders, who were often called judges. The last and the greatest of these figures was Samuel, who heard the people's incessant demand: "Give us a king to judge us like all the other nations have" (1 Samuel 8:5). The Lord reluctantly gave the people what they wanted: a human king.

The Israelites immediately crowned Saul, the tallest

and most impressive of their warriors. The experiment of having a human king didn't work, for Saul wasn't equal to the spiritual demands of leading a nation. David and Solomon, however, came next—and under their leadership Israel became a world power. It was Solomon who extended the empire and built the first Temple.

Solomon was wise, but ultimately weak. He allowed the worship of false gods, and the kingdom began to decay from within. The nation split in two and became easy prey for its conquering neighbors, Assyria and Babylon.

But now all of that was in the past. The only "king" was Herod, who was a puppet of the Romans rather than a prince of his people. Israelite royalty had been brought low since the great days of David and Solomon. Unless one truly trusted the prophecies, it was easy to believe that all the great kings had come and gone.

What about this newborn King, then—the one whose coming was calculated by strange visitors from the East? The star led the wise men away from Jerusalem and toward Bethlehem, which was, of course, where King David had been born. All the same, the Nativity looked like anything but a royal birth. At least David was presumably born in a house, and his father, Jesse, was well-to-do, with a great number of flocks. There had also been Samuel to anoint the shepherd boy's head with oil—the symbol of the Lord's favor and filling.

In contrast, here was a peasant couple and their young son. Even Mary and Joseph must have wondered how a king could rise to power from such humble circumstances. The pageantry of an earthly royal birth would have caught the world's notice.

But God's ways often run counter to our expectations. Jesus didn't arrive in the manner of a king for several reasons, the most important of which is simply that he came to turn the world and its values upside down. The conventional wisdom of our world is that kings rule the rest of us from ivory towers. They set up a hierarchy that ranges from the most powerful to the least. Jesus came to make a shocking statement: that true greatness is found not in ruling but in serving. He built his kingdom not with power but with love. "God blesses those who are humble," he taught, "for they will inherit the whole earth" (Matthew 5:5).

Could Jesus have brought such a message from the window of an imposing palace? Of course not. Jesus was a king incognito—the greatest ruler of all time, in the guise of a poor, traveling teacher. Very few traditional kings embrace lepers or mingle with society's most rejected people.

JESUS WAS A KING INCOGNITO— THE GREATEST RULER OF ALL TIME, IN THE GUISE OF A POOR, TRAVELING TEACHER.

Second, Jesus came to show that the greatest power is to be found not on the outside but in the heart of an individual. He said, "The kingdom of God does not come with observation; nor will they say, 'See here!' or 'See there!' For indeed, the kingdom of God is within you" (Luke 17:20-21, NKJV). As long as power was the exclusive dominion of those who occupied thrones, what hope remained for the poor and the humble? Jesus showed that a blessing lay in the grasp of everyone who loves God, for God loves them and he holds the greatest power of all.

Third, Jesus could not be born as a king because a king would never have been able to pay the price for our sins. Only because he gave up every right of royalty was he able to submit to the death that provided his sacrifice on our behalf.

Pilate, the Roman procurator, recognized some of the tension of the royalty issue when he questioned Jesus. He asked if Jesus was a king. The reply: "My Kingdom is not an earthly kingdom. If it were, my followers would fight to keep me from being handed over to the Jewish leaders. But my Kingdom is not of this world" (John 18:36). The Romans thereafter referred to Jesus as the "King of the Jews" while he was on trial, much to the outrage of those who wanted him killed, and that title was placed on a plaque and nailed above his head as his life drained away on the cross.

The Roman guards laughed at the idea that a "king" could receive the most vicious and dehumanizing of executions. Yet this was entirely the point: The greatest King of all was the one capable of stooping to the lowest level and lifting each of his children toward heaven.

The birth of this King may not have occurred in an opulent setting by human standards. But when our Lord finally stands revealed in all the glory of the next world, every earthly ruler will bow before him. And in that moment, there will be no more greatest or least among mortals—no more princes, no more peasants—only the one eternal King among his beloved, adoring children, who stand hand in hand at the foot of his throne.

Discussion Questions

- Have you ever planned a special occasion for someone else? How did you go about doing it?

- When was the last time you remember a prince or princess being born? How did you learn about it?

For further study: Read 1 Samuel 24:16-20; 2 Samuel 2:1; and 2 Samuel 5:1-3 to see how David became king. What lessons can we learn from David's life?

WHY DO ANNA AND SIMEON CHALLENGE US?

*T*his is a story of faithfulness rewarded, a tale that takes place where happy endings meet hopeful beginnings. Its characters lie neglected on the edges of the Nativity story, just as they were in real life. To find and enjoy this tale is to discover one more gift under the Christmas tree, just when we thought our celebration was complete.

The story begins at the Temple in Jerusalem, one of the world's busiest places. Armies of priests hurry by, attending to sacred tasks. Pilgrims arrive from all points of the compass, eager to see the spectacle and worship the Lord. Here, within the Holy of Holies, dwells the Spirit of God. Only here can he be truly worshiped, will he hear prayers and accept sacrifices.

And here, of course, a number of local eccentrics are always on hand. Every public monument has a few. We tend to ignore these characters, these men like Simeon.

Simeon comes here several times a week. He is drawn

to the Temple almost magnetically by his devotion to God. Through the decades of his life, Simeon has clung to one assurance: that his tired old eyes will look upon the Messiah before they close for the last time. The Spirit of God has whispered this promise to him. Imagine! *He*, Simeon, will behold the Chosen One—and soon. It *must* be soon, because he is old and cannot hold on for much longer.

Friends and relatives have gently reasoned with old Simeon, but he pays no attention to their skepticism. The Messiah will come! And he, Simeon, *will* see him!

For years he has watched and waited. The priests no longer even register his presence. To them, he is just some old man living under a delusion. Let him have his fairy tale, because it gives him something to hang on to.

Today, Simeon cannot suppress his smile. Let people stare, for today is the second time that the Spirit of God has whispered to him. The message: *Go to the Temple, old friend!* So here he comes, creaking along, panting for breath, clacking his walking stick on the polished floor.

As he arrives, Simeon scans the activities at the Temple. For some time he sees nothing unusual. As a matter of fact, when the young couple arrive with their baby boy, he still sees nothing unusual—but he *knows*.

The mother and father have brought their boy for his dedication. By law, all firstborn sons must be presented to God. This one looks like any other infant, but Simeon feels that warm, expansive sensation inside him again— that assurance that can only be the Holy Spirit. It bestows the sight that does not come through eyes; it tells his heart what it yearns to hear.

Simeon hurries to the little family's side, clutching his

walking stick with both hands. The parents seem startled by his attention, but slowly they relax. Joseph steps back as Mary smiles and gently offers her child to Simeon.

The old man gazes in adoration at the soft, vulnerable bundle in his arms. A tear begins to wander through the deep wrinkles of his cheeks. When he holds the child aloft with trembling hands, bolstered by Joseph, the words begin to flow from him. They gush forth in such a way that they become a song, and all in the Temple stop to hear it.

> *"Sovereign Lord, now let your servant die in peace,*
>   *as you have promised.*
> *I have seen your salvation,*
>   *which you have prepared for all people.*
> *He is a light to reveal God to the nations,*
>   *and he is the glory of your people Israel!"*
>   *Luke 2:29–32*

On this day, pilgrims and priests and passersby stare at Simeon as if seeing him for the first time. His melodious words bear a power and an authority no one has ever suspected—especially as he delicately returns the child to his mother. As Simeon does so, it is as if an invisible cloud has blotted out the sunshine that is the old man's countenance.

Simeon is speaking gravely to Mary, and only those within a few feet can hear. It is about the Child being beloved by many but rejected by others, about the Child's ability to lay bare the truth of every human creature. His final prophetic comment brings a visible tremble to the mother.

And just then, the second part of the story unfolds. A woman comes upon the scene and begins worshiping God in a loud voice. All the "regulars" know her: It is Anna, who is eighty-four years old and thought to be a prophetess. Some, like Simeon, frequent the Temple; Anna never leaves it. For years it has been her whole world, and people sense that no one could be closer to God than someone who has dwelt for so many years in close proximity to the holiest place on earth.

THE JOYFUL MESSAGE COMES THROUGH CHANNELS NO ONE EXPECTED— NOT THROUGH THE PRIESTS OR THE CROWD FAVORITES BUT THROUGH TWO OLD, FORGOTTEN RELICS OF GOOD OLD-TIME RELIGION.

They say Anna was once married. But her husband died before most of these people were even born. How many firstborn dedications has she witnessed? Yet she has never responded like this! What Simeon seems to know, she publishes abroad. She is telling everyone in the room that the Messiah has come. She tells about the future works of Jesus—God himself, the Lord of lords, speaking through this faded, elderly woman! Mary and Joseph are smiling again, even laughing. Simeon is laughing, too, and weeping.

For years people will relive this remarkable day at the Temple. The joyful message comes through channels no one expected—not through the priests or the crowd favorites but through two old, forgotten relics of good old-time religion.

It comes to them simply because they have been faithful. And one more message resonates through this Nativity story that is filled with messages—the moral being that God rewards the faithful. The Christ child is a gift to all, to those in the past as well as the future. But those who know him will tell you that some of the greatest joys of all are imparted to the wise, faithful servants that the rest of us overlook.

Discussion Questions

◌ Can you think of a person who has shown exceptional patience and dependability? Who? Why?

◌ What would you do if someone showed so much attention to your newborn? Why?

For further study: Each of the following gives a promise to those who are faithful. Read each passage and identify the blessing it tells of: Proverbs 28:20; Colossians 1:2; 2 Timothy 2:11-13; and Revelation 2:10.

WHY DO WE CELEBRATE CHRISTMAS ON DECEMBER 25?

*W*e often think of the Nativity as the "first Christmas." But was it? It depends upon what is meant by the word *Christmas*.

If we mean the birthday of Christ, then no other day is the first Christmas. But that's not what the word *Christmas* actually means. It comes down to us from a Middle English term, *Christemasse,* the "Christ mass," or Christ's service of worship.

But does that celebration fall on his actual date of birth? No one can know for certain. For hundreds of years, scholars have attempted to solve this puzzle. We do know that Jesus was born sometime around 4 BC. (Yes, it's surprising when we consider that *BC* means "before Christ"; the fact is that when our present calendar was first organized, an error of several years was made.)

Was Christ born "in the bleak midwinter"? Possibly so.

A few interesting theories point to his birth on the very day we designate. Others, however, mention the fact that shepherds were keeping watch over their flocks by night, as Luke tells us. That would suggest a springtime date, although if these were Temple sheep, destined to be used as sacrifices, they would have been on the hillsides year round. The early Christian leaders, living only a century or two after Jesus, honored the date of March 25, which they set as the vernal equinox—an important day for the farming-based ancients.

But why weren't believers celebrating the birth of their Lord from the beginning? Official "holy days," or what we now call holidays, tend to evolve only as they become set traditions. Besides, not all the early Christian leaders were in favor of institutionalizing their faith. Origen, an early theologian, spoke out against celebrating the birthday of Jesus in AD 245. Sinners, not saints, celebrate birthdays, he said.

But as the years passed, March 25 remained a focal point of the calendar. During the Middle Ages, this date emerged as the time for the Feast of Annunciation. That was a commemoration of Gabriel's visit to Mary, telling her the wonderful news of Christ's coming birth. Medieval and Renaissance painters loved painting this scene, with the magnificent angel standing before Mary.

As church traditions continued to be established throughout medieval times, people wanted to celebrate the Nativity itself. It stood to reason that such a day would fall nine months after Gabriel made his proclamation, which everyone connected with March 25. They did the math and came up with December 25, which was the winter solstice. Therefore December 25 became the traditional date for celebrating the Christ Mass.

Other factors influenced the connection between Christmas and December 25. The date was often used for Roman feasting and celebration. In the beginning, of course, Christians and Romans had little in common. But by the time of Constantine, those two designations became almost synonymous. In the West, Christianity was the "Roman Church." It was inevitable that, just as Christian influences spread into Roman lands, Roman influences found their way into Christianity.

In the end, December 25 became just what it is today: a holiday that mixes the sacred and the secular. In Constantine's time, there was celebration of the Roman god Mithras occurring as the birthday of Christ was observed; today, worship is in competition with the modern "gods" of sports and materialism. There is an undying tension between the Christian and the non-Christian elements that compete for our attention during the last month of the year.

On the other hand, we need not worry about Mithras; the worship of that god barely outlived the emperor Constantine. The old Roman and pagan festivals all passed away, too. In time, the name of Christ stamped itself upon the holiday: *Christmas.* Christian leaders decided to use this period of the annual calendar to emphasize that Christ was fully human and fully divine.

By AD 336, there were Christmas celebrations in Rome itself. The Child, who had come so quietly into a stable in the Middle East, had conquered the capital of the world's greatest empire in only three centuries. As each Christmas came and went, he would continue to move throughout the world, healing, teaching, and changing hearts. His voice would be heard and his ministry felt wherever his followers traveled. And indeed they traveled.

THE CHILD,
WHO HAD COME
SO QUIETLY
INTO A STABLE
IN THE MIDDLE
EAST, HAD
CONQUERED
THE CAPITAL OF
THE WORLD'S
GREATEST EMPIRE
IN ONLY THREE
CENTURIES.

Followers of Christ colonized the farthest reaches of Western Europe, then across the Atlantic to America, on to Africa and South America, into the heart of China and everywhere people live and need a Savior.

Today, on the twenty-fifth of December each year, you can hear Christmas carols being sung on every populated continent as the sun works its way from east to west. You will hear the carols in a thousand languages and dialects. The same, beloved Nativity story will be recounted over and over again, from the visit of Gabriel to the treachery of Herod. Children will portray shepherds and wise men. Television specials and magazine covers will ask again, "Who was the man from Nazareth who lived two thousand years ago, and who still inspires such love and obedience?" Just as those early church leaders desired, we will set aside this time to reason together about how God became human and how humans came back to God.

And yes, we would love to know exactly what day and what year marked the birth, what latitude and what longitude marked the stable, what country of origin provided the wise men, what number of angels populated the skies, and what galaxy housed the star of Bethlehem. But upon further consideration, we realize that we know all we need to know. After all, the time of Christ's birth is now, this very second, within each of us. He continues to smile upon us from the crude mangers of our souls every moment that we feel his love, and particularly when we give that love away.

And December 25? It's as good a day as any. It's a "together day" when we can feel all the world bowing as one before the King. But all the other days of the year are Christmas, too. That's the measure of his great gift to us.

Discussion Questions

◎ What is your favorite Christmas tradition? Why?

◎ Does it matter to you that the actual date of Jesus' birthday might be different from December 25? Why or why not?

For further study: Read Romans 5:1-11. List the many gifts that we receive because of our faith in Jesus' nativity and his sacrificial life.

WHY DID JESUS COME?

*A*s the moon lit the treetops and the evening breeze cooled her skin, Mary rested quietly, renewing her strength. She gazed in wonder at the tiny, living gift in her arms. Any child, of course, is a miracle from heaven—a firstborn in particular.

Even so, Mary understood that the child she held was set apart from any other that had ever been born. She knew what the angel had told her and what her heart confirmed: *Here at my breast is the Son of God.* Those were the very words, the very designation, the angel had given: *Son of God* (see Luke 1:35).

Yet the question was, *Why?*

We can imagine Joseph standing proudly at his wife's shoulder. He would be keeping watch—standing guard, as fathers do. Joseph must have glanced at the moonlit clouds and pondered his own mysteries. The information supplied to the engaged couple had been very limited. Exactly what was the Lord doing in this small town, on this quiet night, in this obscure province? When God invaded human affairs, the very earth should tremble. But here was a scene one might find anywhere in the world: a mother, a father, an infant.

Why was heaven so preoccupied with a scene so unremarkable?

Joseph did what we would have done. He returned again and again to what he himself had experienced. He carefully sifted the words of his own angelic visitor. The messenger had said, "You are to name him Jesus, for he will save his people from their sins" (Matthew 1:21).

The words of angels are not likely to be forgotten. They are memorized, cherished, inscribed upon the heart, and shared only with the most intimate friends. Mary and Joseph each had their visit from an angel, and each held their piece of the puzzle. Mary had been told who the baby was, while Joseph had been told what he would do.

As the child increased in wisdom and in stature, can we doubt that his parents shared the angels' words over and over?

You are the Son of God.

You will save your people from their sins.

How old was the child before such mysteries were entrusted to his reflection? The God of heaven, the source of the messages, surely guided them at every crossroad. His will came to Jesus by way of angels, then parents, then the young man's own encounters with his true Father.

It's not surprising, then, that we find a young man in the Gospels who speaks frequently of his mission. His very first recorded words were to tell his parents they should have expected him to be involved in his Father's business (see Luke 2:49).

Even so, Luke tells us that his parents didn't understand his words. What was his Father's business? Who was this young boy with a twelve-year-old body and an ageless wisdom? We can imagine the whispered conversations between Mary and Joseph late at night. Why had Jesus come? And when the time arrived—as inevitably it must—where would he go? What would he do? Would the world finally understand the incredible secret held only between heaven and one small family?

When the day of fulfillment came, some three decades after his birth, Jesus had been given many years to wrestle with the identity told to Mary and the mission told to Joseph. We can imagine that he spoke often with those two. He discoursed with the local teachers. He pored over the words of the prophets until they were part of his very being. *I am the one Isaiah described so long ago.*

THERE MUST HAVE BEEN MOMENTS WHEN HE MOURNED THE LOSS OF THE SIMPLE LIFE, THE COMMON LIFE—THE LIFE OF MARRIAGE AND CHILDREN AND GRAND-CHILDREN— THAT HE KNEW HE MUST NOT CHOOSE.

There must have been moments when he mourned the loss of the simple life, the common life—the life of marriage and children and grandchildren— that he knew he must not choose. But his heart was true. When he knew the time was right, he journeyed deep into the wilderness alone, denying himself food and water. There, in solitude, identity and mission came together for him. There Jesus himself confronted the temptations of the devil, and he mastered them.

And when he emerged, we find that Jesus was constantly answering the great question—why had he come? On thirteen occasions in the short Gospel records, he used the phrase, "I have come . . .".

I have come to call . . . sinners. (Matthew 9:13)
I have come . . . in my Father's name. (John 5:43)
I have come . . . to do the will of God. (John 6:38)
I come from him, and he sent me to you.
    (John 7:29)
I have come as a light to shine in this dark world.
    (John 12:46)

If the written record is any clue, no sense of mission has ever burned brighter. Ordinary people never speak of "coming" to this world; this world is *home*. Jesus employed the language of a guest. He spoke in the parlance of an ambassador on a short but urgent assignment.

Perhaps his most moving purpose statement came on the day when he encountered a strange little man named Zacchaeus. The latter was a man of wealth and distinction. Yet when Jesus passed through town, the little man ran ahead of the crowd and climbed into the branches of a tree. His lack of dignity was appalling, but people tended to avert their eyes from Zacchaeus anyway. After all, he had made his fortune by tapping into the corruption of Roman taxation. Conventional wisdom said that a noble teacher of godly truth should ignore such a public parasite.

But imagine—Jesus called the little man by name, then suggested the two should share a meal at the tax collector's home. In the eyes of the crowd, it was a serious misstep for Jesus, and they made their opinions known. Jesus said, "I, the Son of Man, have come to seek and save those like him who are lost" (see Luke 19:10).

To seek and to save the lost. There is music and majesty in that statement. One focus: *the lost.* Two actions: *seek and save.* The ambassador's urgent business, then, is a rescue mission.

Seek and save. We think of pictures of sailors clinging to the wreckage of a ship. Helicopters hover in the night sky, shining their beacons on the sea in search of the living who must be saved. We think of a collapsed mine, where workers are trapped far beneath the earth. Their oxygen runs low, and the men crouch in darkness, wondering if they dare hope for salvation. We think of a little girl at the bottom of a well, or even the favorite word picture of a single stray sheep trapped on a perilous outcropping. One animal in a flock of hundreds, and who would miss it? The shepherd would. He will leave the many to find the one, at any cost.

The coast guard will find those three or four bobbing sailors, and no taxpayer will complain about the expense. The miners will not be abandoned, and the little girl must see the sunshine once more. These situations are urgent, and when they come across our television screens, everyone stops and prays and waits.

When those New York Fire Department workers

rushed into the rubble of the World Trade Center, they never stopped to ask about the risks. They pushed forward, fully willing to pay the highest price life can demand. The idea of rescue is at the core of our being; it stops us in our tracks.

But the true tragedy transcends the occasional current event. Now, as ever, the world lies in its own rubble, its own self-inflicted darkness and pain. The greatest enemy of all is the irresistible force within us, the thing known in the Bible as *sin*. We are all too aware of its grip upon us. We know that its only work is that of our destruction. And yet we enslave ourselves to it in every way. No one has the power to rise above the tendrils of sin. Therefore the ruin of our fallen state is all around us. The debris is all-pervasive. Our world's inhabitants, billions of them, long for their rescue, often without even realizing what that longing is for.

WHEN THOSE NEW YORK FIRE DEPARTMENT WORKERS RUSHED INTO THE RUBBLE OF THE WORLD TRADE CENTER, THEY NEVER STOPPED TO ASK ABOUT THE RISKS.

Then a light shines in the darkness. A beacon slashes through our despair.

It is Jesus. He stands among us and says, "I have come to seek and to save the lost—to find you and to restore you."

The word *gospel* means "good news," and that is surely the understatement of the cosmos. The news is so good, so outrageously wonderful, that the world finds it difficult to believe. *A cure has been discovered for the common sin.* Death itself now has an alternative—and the alternative will be so good that on the day we experience it our feeble minds could never contain the joy involved.

But it only gets better.

Jesus made another "I come" statement. The primary reason was a rescue mission. Jesus also mentioned a secondary goal. He said, "My purpose is to give them a rich and satisfying life" (John 10:10). When he said those words, he was talking about sheep again. He said that a false shepherd simply uses the sheep; a true shepherd loves them enough to give his life for them. "I have come not only to rescue you," he was saying, "but to help you see all the wonderful possibilities that life can hold for you. I want you to squeeze every single drop of joy out of this life. And if I didn't come to show you, you would never know how."

Mary was told that her child would be the Son of God. Joseph was told that this child would save his people from their sins. These were the two greatest imaginable statements concerning the infant. But how could the angels possibly have explained all that those two ideas entailed? How can you explain a rainbow to those who have lived in a world of gray?

Perhaps the angels themselves couldn't have anticipated the miracle of Jesus—the sheer wonder of the light that was about to break forth upon the earth like a heavenly sunrise after thousands of years of night. We are more fortunate, for we have his words. We have the testament of his life. Best of all, we have the experience of knowing what life can be in all its fullness—as wonderful as Jesus promised it would be.

Discussion Questions

    ℰ Have you ever gone on a mission trip? What was
your motivation?

    ℰ Based on what you read in this chapter, what was
Jesus' prime motivation for coming to earth?

For further study: This chapter covers six of the thirteen
times Jesus said "I have come." Read the following passages to find more of the reasons Jesus gave for coming:
Matthew 5:17; Matthew 20:28; and John 17:8.

WHY MUST JESUS COME AGAIN?

$\mathcal{T}$he discussion continued for many generations. The subject: redemption. It was all about the Promised One who would finally arrive to correct everything that was wrong. The speakers were the prophets, those timeless visionaries among the people of God.

Sometimes their conversation took the form of poetry, expressing deep emotions of hope and yearning. They urged, "Come, O King! Come without delay!" Other times they uttered grim descriptions of the judgment that awaited God's enemies. And there were times when they offered specific, remarkably accurate details of the one who was to come.

Prophets are people who can see further than the rest of us. So imagine, if you will, that what the prophets were seeing from such a great distance was a towering mountain peak. The Messiah's coming, after all, would represent the loftiest point in human history. The prophets could see through the mist of time. They were giving details of what they could make out.

But then, as they grew closer to that time and that "mountain," the prophets realized that what they had thought was one great peak was actually two of them—with a great valley in between. In other words, the Messiah would appear among his people not once but twice, and our era of history is the valley that lies between his two comings.

Isaiah, Jeremiah, Micah, and the others knew there would be a Messiah, and they even gathered some of the details. But they didn't realize he would come twice. The writers who came after Jesus—Paul and Peter, for example—had a closer vantage point. They were able to understand the First Coming of Jesus, because he had come in their time. And while Jesus was among us, he said he would make one more visit, at which time he would fulfill the remaining prophecies—the ones about a triumphant conqueror, coming to usher in a perfect kingdom.

The first appearance of Jesus was a mission of humility and sacrifice. He came to deal with the problem of our sin once and for all. The second appearance will be a mission of triumph and transformation. And what will it be like? Listen to Isaiah's description:

> *The government will rest on his shoulders. And he will be called: Wonderful Counselor, Mighty God, Everlasting Father, Prince of Peace. His government and its peace will never end. He will rule with fairness and justice from the throne of his ancestor David for all eternity. The passionate*

> *commitment of the LORD of Heaven's Armies will*
> *make this happen!*   Isaiah 9:6-7

Don't we all long for such a world?

However, we must ask the question: If Jesus conquered death on his first visit, why must he come again?

The most important reason is that he plans to come back to claim his people, so that he can take them home with him forever. As Jesus discussed his intention, he often used the word picture of a groom returning for his bride. The church, he said, is the "bride of Christ." The bride waits eagerly for her new husband to come and claim her like a knight on a lovely stallion, taking her home to her "happily ever after." That home, of course, is heaven; and the marriage is the ultimate intimacy with Christ that all his people will share, never to be separated from him again.

He will arrive for us in the sky, just as he left when he ascended to heaven. According to 1 Thessalonians 4:16-17, he will break through the clouds with a great shout and the voice of an archangel. A trumpet will sound, and those of his children who have passed away will rise to meet him. Then his living followers will join them, and all of them will return to live with Christ forever.

Second, he must come again to judge the world. Jesus spoke several times of the final judgment, when he would come to judge the living and the dead and to separate his faithful children from those who refused to follow him. People throughout history who have placed their faith in God will be declared innocent, every sin forgiven, because they have accepted the sacrifice of Christ. Others will pay the terrible price of their rebellion.

Third, Jesus Christ will return to establish "a new heaven and a new earth" (Revelation 21:1). The old will have passed away as Christ draws the final curtain on

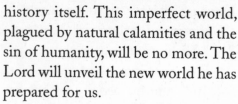

history itself. This imperfect world, plagued by natural calamities and the sin of humanity, will be no more. The Lord will unveil the new world he has prepared for us.

WE CAN'T IMAGINE SUCH A LIFE: THERE WILL BE NO MORE SIN, NO MORE PAIN, AND NO MORE TEARS.

In that world, everything will be a fresh creation. It will be the eternal kingdom of God, where all his people will live in perfect fellowship with one another and with their Lord. We can't imagine such a life; there will be no more sin, no more pain, and no more tears.

This new Jerusalem, as the book of Revelation calls it, will be a world of perpetual joy—in short, the life we were created to have with God all along. As Paul stated so well, "Now we see things imperfectly as in a cloudy mirror, but then we will see everything with perfect clarity" (1 Corinthians 13:12). Indeed the Bible teaches that we will still have bodies, but perfected "resurrection bodies." If we could truly grasp the tiniest sliver of understanding of heaven's reality, we would have no fear of death.

But what can we do here and now? We can be ready, because the Bible has warned us that Jesus will return unexpectedly, in the blink of an eye, "like a thief in the night" (1 Thessalonians 5:2). The best way to be ready is to become consumed by lives of loving and serving Jesus.

Wouldn't it be wonderful to be "caught in the act" of obedience at his return?

Jesus would smile, beckon to us, and say, "Well done, good and faithful servants. Enter now into the reward I have prepared for you."

Discussion Questions

□ According to this chapter, what will be the sights and sounds of the Second Coming of Christ?

□ Which of the reasons that Jesus must come again presented in this chapter gives you the most hope? Which causes the most discomfort? Why?

For further study: Read Titus 2:11-15, looking for mention of both of the comings of Jesus. List three things this passage tells us to do as we await the Second Advent of Jesus.

WHY DO I NEED TO
BELIEVE IN JESUS?

So there we have it: the Nativity. Who could argue that it's a wonderful story?

If you've come this far in our journey, you've probably learned a number of facts about the event. You understand more about those wise men from the East and why they made their journey. You have a good idea what kind of young man Joseph was, and why Mary was God's choice to be the mother of Jesus. You've learned why Herod raged, the shepherds obeyed, and the angels praised.

There are only so many facts for us to cherish concerning the Nativity. Beyond the information in the Bible, there's little more to tell. The real question is this: What now?

If you had just read a biography of Caesar Augustus, the answer would be simple. It would be time to go to the bookshelf and choose another book. The Roman emperor has been dead for quite some time, and he has little true relevance for our daily lives. The facts of his life are intriguing, but there's nothing we can really *do* with them.

The Nativity story is a different matter. The obscure birth of a peasant child, seemingly insignificant in its time, reaches across the years to command our attention. It suggests importance not just for those who were involved in the events, but for all the rest of us, even from a distance of twenty centuries. We can almost feel the gaze of that child in the stable, looking deep into our eyes and demanding a response. But what kind of a response? And why should the birth of Jesus bear any more claim upon us than any other event?

The story of Jesus is an all-encompassing one. It is ultimately not a narrative about its own time, but one about *all* time. It is not simply about Mary, Joseph, Herod, and the others. It concerns us just as if we had stood beside those shepherds that night, knelt by the manger, and marveled at the newborn child.

Why do you and I need to believe in Jesus today?

First, we should believe in him because he believes in us. Jesus was God in flesh. He loved us all along with an overwhelming passion that expressed itself most powerfully in his presence among us, even though that meant he had to limit himself to the frailty and weakness of human existence. He was willing to make himself the least powerful among us, though he held in his hand total command of the universe. He believed in us enough to temporarily lay aside his rights of divinity, so that he might appear in our midst as a human being who was like us in every way.

Yes, he believes in us, and we can feel it. We look around us and realize this world must have been created by Someone who loves us. As Paul phrases it,

> Ever since the world was created, people have seen the earth and sky. Through everything God made, they can clearly see his invisible qualities—his eternal power and divine nature.
>
> *Romans 1:20*

We see it all around us, but we feel it within us, too. Every one of us is painfully aware of our terrible limitations—a hopeless compulsion to say and do and even think the wrong things. Even so, we feel God calling to us, deep within the part of us we call the soul. Surely there is Someone far greater than our weakness, Someone who loves us and wants us to know a better life. He believes in us, so is it really so difficult to believe in him?

Second, we should believe in him because he invites us to a life that makes sense. Through his teachings, Jesus showed us the only workable strategy for living a happy and fulfilling life in this world. He spoke of living by love and unselfishness rather than the inevitable emptiness of self-seeking. He showed us that when we devote ourselves to one another and to serving one another, life is fuller and more satisfying. Ever since the coming of Christ, billions of people have lived according to his pattern and found it to be the way to joy and peace.

Even though the way of Jesus is perfectly rational and clearly the best approach, the world never acknowledges it. We are molded by our culture to live in a way that is totally opposed to the way of Christ. The conventional wisdom is that we should look out for our own interests, give only if it will help us receive, and gratify the appetite rather than the soul. That way leads to self-destruction and despair, yet most people continue to choose it because our human condition dictates that experience. We are fallen creatures who, when left to our own devices, go against the grain of God's truth for us.

THE CONVENTIONAL WISDOM IS THAT WE SHOULD LOOK OUT FOR OUR OWN INTERESTS, GIVE ONLY IF IT WILL HELP US RECEIVE, AND GRATIFY THE APPETITE RATHER THAN THE SOUL.

Yet every element of the story of Christ, from his birth to his ascension, shows us that life need not be empty, that we need not live in perpetual conflict with our neighbors, and that the simplest things in life can be joyful and fulfilling.

Third, we should believe in Jesus because he lives today and because he longs to live within us. The shepherds and wise men enjoyed a wonderful privilege in beholding Jesus face-to-face. The disciples were given quite a gift in hearing the teachings of Jesus in person. But you and I have something even more wonderful. Jesus is just as alive today as he was in the first century, and we can have a much closer relationship with him than those who knew him when he walked the earth.

When it came time for him to leave this world, Jesus

told the disciples that it was actually an advantage to them that he leave. It meant the Holy Spirit would come to live within all those who believe in Jesus. That Spirit would represent the presence of Christ within us. Jesus said, "When the Father sends the Advocate as my representative—that is, the Holy Spirit—he will teach you everything and will remind you of everything I have told you" (John 14:26).

The Holy Spirit makes a dynamic difference in everyday life. He guides us toward the truth, he gently shows us our areas of sin, and he encourages us when our spirits are low. He gradually draws us toward the right choices in life, in the smaller issues as well as the larger ones. We are never alone, nor are we left to our own limited resources, if Christ has become our Lord and Savior; the Holy Spirit makes his home within us permanently.

Finally, we should believe in Jesus because only through him can we find forgiveness for every sin—past, present, and future—and thus live with the hope of eternal life. Why can't we be forgiven and admitted to heaven any other way? The truth is that God is holy, righteous, and perfect. There can be no shadow of imperfection in his sight. We are fallen in every aspect, and even when we try to live positive and helpful lives, we can't change the fact that sin permeates our being. Because God is just and must judge sin, we would never stand a chance of avoiding that judgment no matter how hard we tried or how many good deeds we attempted.

Only one human being has ever lived a perfect and sinless life—Jesus. Yet in submitting to the Cross, he was willing to take the punishment we have earned. It is an exchange. Because a righteous man took a sinner's punishment, a sinner could receive the righteous man's reward. Jesus made that sacrifice for every single one of us. He paid the price for every sin, so that we can reap the benefit of what he earned through his perfect life.

EVERY POSSIBLE FACET OF TRUSTING JESUS IS AN EXCITING ONE. HE OFFERS US ALL THAT COULD POSSIBLY BE GOOD IN LIFE, AND HE FREES US FROM THE SLAVERY OF DEATH AND DESPAIR.

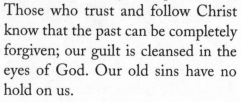

Those who trust and follow Christ know that the past can be completely forgiven; our guilt is cleansed in the eyes of God. Our old sins have no hold on us.

That being the case, death, too, has lost its power over us. Paul the apostle offers us this hope concerning the grave that awaits every human being: "Our dying bodies must be transformed into bodies that will never die; our mortal bodies must be transformed into immortal bodies" (1 Corinthians 15:53). We should believe in Jesus because he is our one and only hope of forgiveness in this world and of joyful existence in the next.

Every possible facet of trusting Jesus is an exciting one. He offers us all that could possibly be good in life, and he frees us from the slavery of death and despair. Therefore the question finally becomes a personal one: Do *you* believe in Jesus? And if not, are you willing to step forward and make that commitment now? The gift is free, and all that is required from you is your sincere acknowledgment and acceptance of it before God.

How, then, would you make that acknowledgment? You would need only to speak with him from your heart. You could offer a prayer, in your own words, that might sound something like this:

> *Jesus, I believe in you. I know that you have loved me from the beginning, and now I choose to love you, too. I realize that when you died, you had my sins in mind. I cannot live a life of joy and peace apart from you. So I accept the gift of your forgiveness, and I rejoice that my debt of sin is paid in full! Come into my life, and guide me for the rest of my days. I now belong completely to you, and I will follow you as my Lord and my Savior forever. Amen.*

Did you pray that prayer, or one like it? If so, the moment you asked Christ to come into your life, it happened—that is a certainty. The Holy Spirit has come to live within you, and you will gradually learn to hear his voice. You may not feel any overwhelming emotion at this time, but the solid fact of your becoming a child of Christ is not dependent upon any emotion.

As a new believer, you will also want to let someone know about your commitment. Find a good church where there will be friends to support and encourage you. Life's greatest adventure lies ahead, and each day will be richer and more joyful as you become more acquainted with the life and the lordship of Christ, which all began at the Nativity.

Discussion Questions

⊘ Have you ever prayed a prayer like the one at the end of this chapter? When? What details can you recall about it?

⊘ Whom do you know who needs to know this truth? What will you do to tell them?

For further study: Read the following passages and list other reasons why we need to believe in Jesus: John 10:9; John 14:6; Acts 4:12; and 1 Timothy 2:5.

ABOUT THE AUTHOR

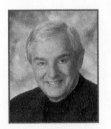

$\mathscr{D}$R. DAVID JEREMIAH is the senior pastor of Shadow Mountain Community Church in El Cajon, California. He is also the founder of Turning Point, a ministry committed to providing sound Bible teaching through international radio and television broadcasting. Dr. Jeremiah has authored numerous books, including the best-selling *What in the World Is Going On?*, *Captured by Grace*, *Life Wide Open*, *My Heart's Desire*, and *Sanctuary*. He and his wife, Donna, have four children and ten grandchildren.